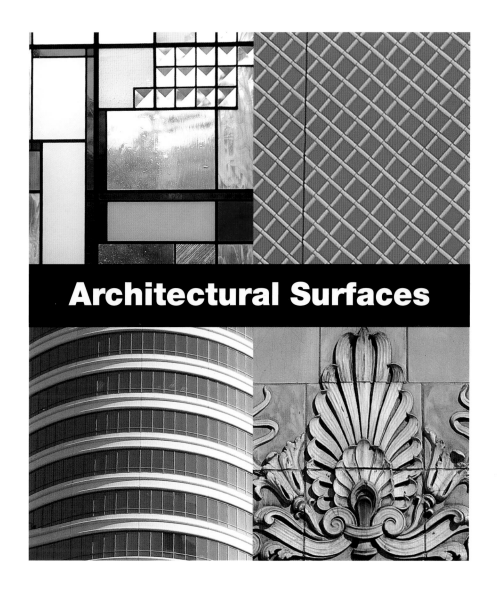

Architectural Surfaces

Architectural Surfaces

Details for Architects, Designers and Artists

Judy A. Juracek

Thames & Hudson

First published in the United Kingdom in 2005 by
Thames & Hudson Ltd, 181A High Holborn,
London WC1V 7QX
1005347402
www.thamesandhudson.com

British Library Cataloguing-in-Publication Data
A catalogue record for this book is available from the British Library

ISBN-13: 978-0-500-34218-3

ISBN-10: 0-500-34218-0

Printed and bound in Hong Kong

CONTENTS

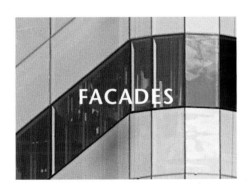

WALLS

FACADES

ORNAMENT & MOLDING

COLUMNS, POSTS & ARCHES

FOREWORD
by Peter Pennoyer

With *Architectural Surfaces*, Judy Juracek completes the fourth volume in her series of collections of images of the natural and manmade world that offer incredibly illuminating views of what things look like. The books are subtitled "Visual Research" and "Details" for artists, architects, and designers. In fact, *Architectural Surfaces* is much more than a research tool, capturing a vast catalog of architectural features in crisp, revealing photographs. As a tool for architects, interior designers, set designers, and related professionals, this book is useful on many levels.

Catalogs of flora and fauna lend themselves to a clear organizational structure. Each species has certain qualities that distinguish it from others. Guides to trees, birds, and animals appear almost every year. But to catalog architectural elements is clearly more ambitious and requires the author to venture into a field where personal judgment replaces taxonomy. In *American Architecture Since 1780*, Marcus Wiffen describes forty styles while admitting that each has "an almost limitless capacity for hybridization." *Architectural Surfaces* allows the individual qualities of each subject to stand out while suggesting its relationship to architecture as a whole.

Juracek has managed to bring a useful degree of order to this extraordinary catalog of images. But the categories in the book serve as a gentle guide and never seem to prevent pleasing visual segues. Our eyes move from Japanese stone post bases to Ionic plinths in a layout that enhances their shared qualities. She achieves this balance by keeping her abstract knowledge of architecture and materials in the background and relying more on her artistic eye.

Architects and designers have long collected their own libraries of important images. Students at the Ecole des Beaux-Arts in Paris—the greatest architecture school in the world from 1850 to 1950—would embark on the grand tour, traveling south through Italy to view, measure, and draw the great monuments of history and often the less celebrated vernacular structures. Their sketchbooks became a tool for future reference and a basis of many great practices. The images also served to make other, more academic sources more accessible and real. The great Renaissance buildings in the drawings in Paul Letarouilly's *Edifices de Rome Moderne* come alive when one views them with a key to the textures and colors and physicality of the actual buildings.

As soon as photographs of architecture became available, architects and designers realized their potential as mnemonic devices. Charles Platt, the artist who became an architect in 1890, did not have the benefit of an education at the Ecole des Beaux-Arts, but he did travel throughout Europe with his brother, assembling a vast collection of photographs (some taken with his own camera, others purchased) that became the core of his office library. These images were organized in bound volumes by subject—fountains, vaults, ceilings, etc.—not in any historical or academic order. The volumes, though well worn and faded, survive today as an early attempt by a designer to capture reminders of what things look like. Yet even Platt's catalog covers only a fraction of the world Juracek has assembled in *Architectural Surfaces*.

Each photograph in this book records the physical qualities of its subject: if it is stone, we see the texture, color, grain, and shape. These basic attributes are what we would expect in any catalog, but here we see more. Juracek's lens suggests those qualities that animate the image: the moment and the place, the intensity and angle of the sun, the quality of light, the atmosphere.

One of the most astonishing accomplishments of this book is that the vast number of photographs is, with a few exceptions, taken by the author. Her eye as a photographer is informed by her work as an artist and in sceneography. The continuity of her point of view gives this collection of images a distinct style that while understated, binds them together as one body of work.

At a time when the Internet is becoming more popular as a tool for designers, Juracek's book is a refreshing reminder of the beauty and utility of the printed book. This volume is a welcome addition to the library of resources available to the design world. To page through with a mission—finding one particular kind of wooden siding, for example, is to discover other images that might not have been on the search. This is the unexpected surprise of the book.

Finally, any designer who spends time with this book will discover another, less obvious quality: with these images in hand, one is inspired to look closer at the real world and to notice, as Judy Juracek has done, the essential qualities of the architectural surfaces around us.

ACKNOWLEDGMENTS

A book such as *Architectural Surfaces* demands a wide range of resources, and without the expertise, advice, and generosity of those mentioned here, this book would not have been possible. In addition to expressing my deepest appreciation for their contributions, I must add that meeting and working with these people has been a personally enriching experience.

At the beginning of this project, my editor, Nancy Green, suggested I ask Peter Pennoyer to be the architectural consultant, and I will always be indebted for this suggestion. He has provided an architect's point of view to the structure of the book and to how the pictures were edited and organized. In addition to his careful technical advice, his enthusiasm for the subject and insights into the architecture have contributed much to making the concept of this book become a reality.

Guy Gurney has helped me photograph four books. He not only advised me on techniques, equipment, and film but also assisted me in lighting and shooting locations, and he opened his photo archives to these projects. Many images in the *Surfaces* books would not have found their way to the pages without him.

Others who contributed photographs to this book are Meredith Barchat, Duane Langenwalter, and Peter Miller—all good photographers with a special fondness for finding architectural images.

Judy Proctor of the architecture firm Austin, Patterson, Disston understood the details I was looking for, found examples of them in the firm's project archives, and generously arranged access to those residences. John Winfield also helped me find locations for pictures. Again, The Newport Preservation Society and the Lockwood-Mathews Mansion made available to me the unique architecture found in their properties.

Jean and William Ingram organized my shooting of the extraordinary structures of Bali, gaining permission to photograph Begawan Giri, the Tuga Hotel, and Puri Lumbung. My guide in Bali, Made Murna, had a real knack for finding architectural details. In Tokyo, photographers Kaoru Soehata and Tomoko Shiozawa not only knew what I wanted to shoot, but the best time to take the picture; Nancy Katsura designed an unsurpassed architectural tour of the city. Yukiko Tanisho and Sumiko Nakamura shared their understanding of Kyoto's architecture, and Toshitaka Kitayama and Naoko Wada opened Agon Shu to this book. Elisabeth Newell contributed her perspective and knowledge of architecture in Los Angeles, and Karen and Frank Armitage gave me yet another rich photo itinerary.

The captions were made possible by William West and George de Brigard, and I am indebted to their knowledge and perseverance. Brian Trimbel of the Brick Industry Association provided caption information only available from a professional, as did Andy Banores of O&G Industries. And many thanks to Diane Rich for sharing her skills in reading the captions.

This book is the work of the same team that has produced the rest of the *Surfaces* books, and I can never fully express my appreciation for their skill and dedication. Nancy Green is constant in her support and belief in the books, Leeann Graham continues to carefully guide the production, Bob Elwood's indexes are an extraordinary asset to the series, and Gilda Hannah has, once again, helped me edit the pictures and produced layouts that enhance the images and make the reader want to explore the next page. I am also grateful to Barbara Braun for her assistance, and to Elizabeth Woll for her work in designing the jacket.

INTRODUCTION

A theme-park designer once told me that the most difficult part of designing is getting everything to connect in the corners. She added that anyone with some talent could produce a workable design and draw a handsome elevation, but the skill of a designer was in working out the details. How do courses of brickwork accommodate the shape of an arch? Exactly what happens at the intersection of two stone walls? What is the profile of a molding where a cornice wraps around the corner of a building? Solving these problems with style and elegance is the hallmark of good design; the resulting solutions are the structural and decorative details that are emblematic of historic periods and become the signatures of individual styles and designers.

All artists, including illustrators, animators, and scenic designers, explore architectural details as they render or replicate scenes and environments. Using the correct style of window or appropriate floor and wall finishes often signals the authenticity of the artist's work. Accuracy is particularly important to successful design now, because we have experienced an explosion of visual information, so widely communicated that there are few people who have not been exposed to an extensive file of images. Audiences of all ages, therefore, are visually very sophisticated. They may have acquired this education by osmosis, but they have come to expect believable architecture in everything from film sets and theme parks to the textures found in video game environments.

Architectural Surfaces: Details for Artists, Architects, and Designers is a collection of photographs of architecture, focusing on specific details and elements of buildings. In most cases, organizing the pictures topically was obvious: windows went into one chapter; ceilings and roofs fit nicely into another. However, when it came to walls, it became apparent that the group of images was in danger of being too unwieldy to organize. So, the images are divided into two chapters—"Walls" and "Facades." The first contains subjects made from generally structural materials, such as stone, wood, and brick. The second groups pictures about walls made from materials generally *applied* to a structure, such as glass and metal curtain walls and architectural terracotta. This method of classification sometimes may seem a bit arbitrary, as in the case of stone veneer ("Walls"), which should technically be grouped with other curtain walls ("Facades"). But stone is perceived as a structural material, and the details of coursing and joints in a stone veneer is parallel to that of solid stone construction.

Pictorial research is easier to use if images are filed into specific categories of visually kindred subjects. With this in mind, the chapters are further broken down into sections concentrating on parts of the general topic. For example, "Doorways" is divided into paneled doors, battened doors, painted doors, metal doors, transom lights and side lights, entryways, gates, and door hardware. These categories are not intended to explain the individual parts of a doorway, but to isolate various aspects of doors and entryways in order to present different types and styles within the category.

Within this structure, the index is very much a navigational tool intended to help users find specific architectural details. The subject keywords in the captions are used in the index. Architectural elements tend to overlap categories, and not all examples of a topic are confined to a single chapter. For example, an interesting Palladian window in a photo showing a particular type of roof dormer is located in "Ceilings & Roofs," but the window style is named in the caption and cross-referenced in the index. All entries in the index give an image number that refers both to the picture in the book and to the image on the CD-ROMs.

The captions were compiled with the help of specialists and with additional information from a variety of sources. Since most of the identifications were made only from the photographs, any inaccuracy lies with the author. Most of the architectural terms used in the captions are defined in the glossary.

The images in this book and on the CD-ROMs are the property of the author or the individuals or organizations listed in the photo credits, and may not be used commercially without their express permission.

ADDITIONAL CAPTIONS

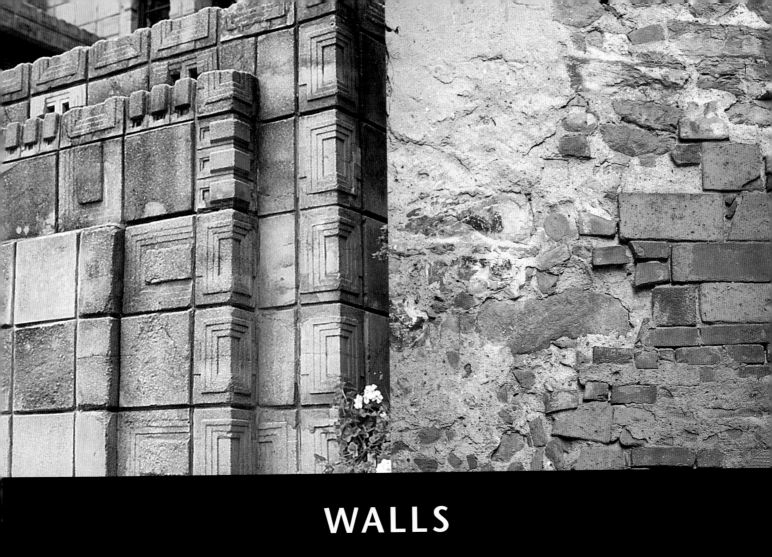

WALLS

Photo: Austin, Patterson, Disston

WA-1 Interior applied cherry-veneered panels with square finished edges on painted wood frame

WA-2 Weathered cedar-paneled entry screen. Top: notched vertical boards; bottom: herringbone pattern

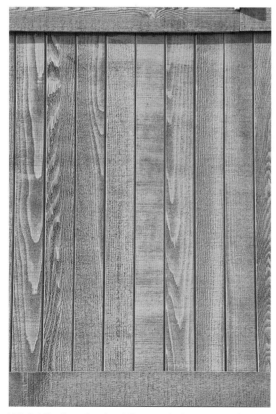

WA-3 Weathered cedar siding, vertical tongue-and-groove

WA-4 Stained and sealed board-and-batten siding

WA-5 Pine log house construction, corner detail

WA-6 Plain-sawn vertical planks with decorative battens

WA-7 Knotty-cedar flush, vertical plain-sawn board wall, with horizontal batten divider

WA-8 Batten door (left); shutter behind diagonally split square-stock wood bars (upper right); elm waney-edged clapboard bottom (lower right) on an outbuilding

WA-9 Notched corner joint of square timber frame with painted cedar shakes on concrete foundation

WA-10 Timber-frame construction with infill of plain-sawn cedar planks with ceramic ventilation opening

WA-11 Weathered painted wood siding. Left: board-and-batten; right: clapboard

WA-12 Woven bamboo twigs tied to bamboo post and rails, garden fence

WA-13 Woven split-bamboo wall, tropical hut

Photo: Guy Gurney

WA-14 Plain-sawn vertical board fence

WOOD WALLS & SIDING

WA-15 Vertical board siding with new cedar shakes on gable, residential garage

WA-16 Detail of unpainted clapboard and window casing

WA-17 Low entry wall of boxed plain-sawn planks on stone base

WA-18 Entry screen with parquet design

Photo: Austin, Patterson, Disston

WA-19 Framed oiled cedar vertical board paneling,
interior hallway

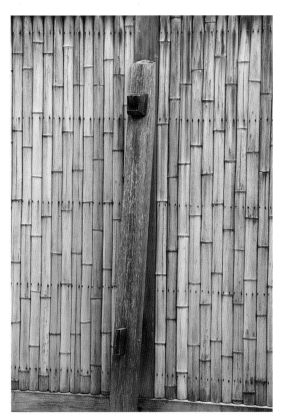

WA-20 Framed bamboo garden wall

WA-21 Antique chestnut interior paneling with mitered
corners and raised panels

WA-22 Painted clapboard gable-end wall with gable ornament and exposed vertical board cladding

WA-23 Weathered clapboard barn with hanging door

WA-24 Unpainted clapboard showing evidence of repair, with double-hung windows, American colonial house

WA-25 Weathered painted clapboard wall with windows

WA-26 Stained and sealed flush vertical board siding on traditional house

WA-27 Weathered board-and-batten siding on outbuilding

WA-28 Gable-end wall with unpainted board-and-batten siding and gable window

WA-29 Dovetail corner and mortar chinking, log house

WA-30 Weathered painted flush vertical board cladding on barn gable end with diamond-shaped window and vertical scallop-edged siding

WA-31 Weathered flush vertical board siding with pediment-capped windows and door, American western saloon facade

WA-32 Painted siding divided by molding. Top to bottom: scalloped wood shingles; board-and-batten; clapboard. Bargeboard with saw-tooth motif

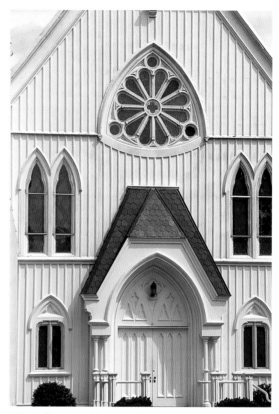

WA-33 Board-and-batten siding with rose window and lancet windows; jerkinhead-roofed entry, Carpenter Gothic church

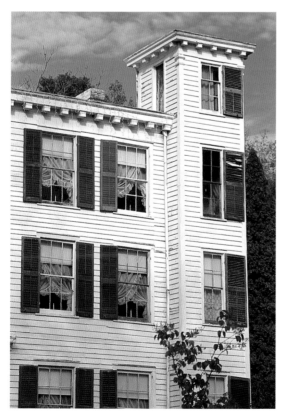

WA-34 Painted clapboard and block modillion cornice on corner tower, Italianate house

WA-35 Clapboard end-gable wall with shuttered gable window, blind window, scalloped rake trim, and pedimented porch, Greek-revival house

WA-36 Weathered untreated clapboard on gambrel-end wall rising from corbel detail

WA-37 Painted colonial clapboard house with wide coner board and a jetty between the first and second stories

WA-38 Painted tongue-and-groove siding on shed-roofed house with corner board and rake trim

WA-39 Painted clapboard siding divided by wide trim, double-hung windows, modillion cornice, and painted shingled roof

WA-40 Tongue-and-groove panels in alternating diagonal patterns, Indonesian house on stilts

WA-41 Timber frame with infill of plain-sawn cedar planks; gutter with rainwater head

WA-42 Stylized half-timber wall with decorative framing over clapboard infill

WA-43 Plain-sawn vertical planks with horizontal batten on shaped stone foundation; timber post with wood base

WA-44 Weathered unfinished plain-sawn planks with vertical undressed timbers on rubble foundation

WA-45 Timber-frame with plain-sawn planks and split-bamboo removable fence

WA-46 Timber frame with infill of planks and battens with sliding doors and paper-covered windows

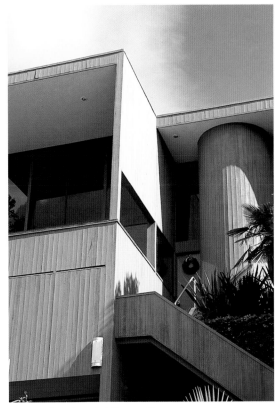

WA-47 Flush board siding on flat and curved surfaces, modern house

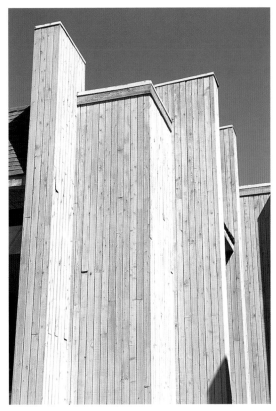

WA-48 Flush board siding, modern commercial building

WA-49 Fortification-style battered wall with lapped-joint corners

WA-50 Stained and sealed vertical siding with second-floor jetty and sliding metal-framed windows, modern house

WOOD WALLS & SIDING

WA-51 Diagonal siding with flat edge trim and corner window, modern house

WA-52 Horizontal stained shiplap siding with corner awning windows, modern house

WA-53 Horizontal and vertical board siding with angled siding aligned to roof rake, modern house

WA-54 Painted vertical board-and-batten siding with corner and base trim on fieldstone foundation

WA-55 Painted horizontal-lattice screened porch on shingle-clad house

WA-56 Split-faced roughly squared sandstone in coursed rubble with ventilation slit

WA-57 Sawn-finish volcanic or pumice stone in running bond

WA-58 Split-faced granite in random ashlar with smooth-faced water-table course, tinted mortar

WA-59 Corner detail of fossil rock in mosaic bond

WA-60 Beach pebbles in coursed rubble with masonry screen window

WA-61 Squared split-faced granite in herringbone pattern

WA-62 Ancient Roman travertine wall in coursed ashlar with sandstone repairs

WA-63 Pool wall in hammered-finish sandstone with mosaic bond and water-line courses of roughly squared stone and beach pebbles

WA-64 Squared rubble with brick course, tinted mortar, dimension-stone quoins, and masonry screen in ogee-arch window, mosque

WA-65 Split- and rock-faced sandstone; shelf course, random ashlar with raked mortar

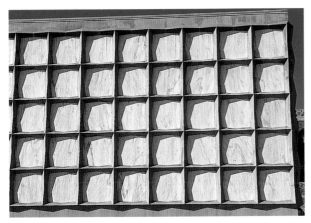

WA-66 Granite veneer on concrete frame with Vermont marble infill, modern commercial building

WA-67 Hammered-finish brownstone in coursed ashlar with flush mortar joints and water-table course

WA-68 Banded sandstone. Top: running bond, honed-finish with rock-face belt course; bottom: running bond, split-face, modern commercial building

WA-69 Pink granite in running bond with polished and flamed finishes forming supergraphic, modern commercial building

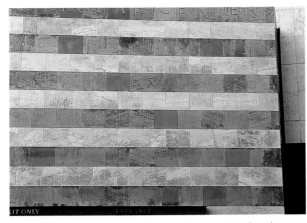

WA-70 Banded white and green marble in running bond, modern commercial building

WA-71 Siena marble in running bond with Vitruvian scroll frieze on hallway wall

WA-72 Coursed ashlar sandstone wall in ruins revealing structural rubble wall

WA-73 Coursed rubble with gallets and rock-face cap

WA-74 Top: fieldstone rubble in mosaic bond; bottom: coursed rubble of beach pebbles

WA-75 Coursed ashlar limestone with sand finish, water-damage weathering

STONE WALLS

WA-76 Massive rubble with gallets, garden wall

WA-77 Roughly squared sandstone in random ashlar attached to natural stone wall

WA-78 Split-faced and rusticated Mexican volcanic stone in running bond, footbridge wall

WA-79 Rubble walls of cobbles with wide squared stone step capping lower wall and coping on upper wall

WA-80 Stone in coursed ashlar with bracket, niche, and perpend under niche, Bali

WA-81 Coursed rubble drywall with pilaster and flagstone coping

STONE WALLS

WA-82 Detail of doorway reveal in stack bond with alternating courses of rock-face and sawn granite; mitered corner joints

WA-83 Corner detail of polished granite veneer with lapped corner joints

WA-84 Edge detail of polished and honed polychrome granite veneers

WA-85 Honed granite veneer in stack bond with grouted joints

WA-86 Sandstone and quartzite in coursed ashlar below herringbone pattern; Indiana limestone ornamented cap

WA-87 Limestone walls. Left: bevel-cut stack bond with jack arch and dentil cornice; right: gem-cut stack bond

WA-88 Polished granite and marble. Left to right: granite-veneer base with bead molding; granite plinth with marble ovolo molding on base; polished granite engaged column

STONE WALLS

WA-89 Honed granite veneer with solid granite base and bead molding beside granite door casing

WA-90 Corner detail of rusticated stone pilaster between banded engaged columns

WA-91 Roughly squared stone in random ashlar wall with flagstone voussoirs in compound arch

WA-92 Sawn ashlar sandstone courses, quoins with vermiculated finish

WA-93 Sawn granite in random ashlar with tooled quoins; flat granite window and base trim

WA-94 Split-faced granite wall in shelf, random ashlar with roughly squared rubble pillar (right)

WA-95 Split-faced granite, coursed ashlar buttresses with water-table course

WA-96 Split-faced coursed roughly squared rubble with sand-finished corbel

STONE WALLS

WA-97 Inside corner of honed-veneer marble in running bond, bottom recently cleaned

WA-98 Outside corner probably of Amherst gray lime-stone, sand-finished in shaped panels

WA-99 Outside corner of split-faced, random ashlar with raised sand-finished quoins and engaged balustrade

WA-100 Partially honed fossil-stone doorway with water-table course and base molding

WA-101 Inside and outside corners in coursed, roughly squared ashlar

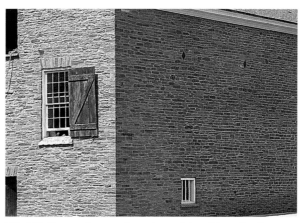

WA-102 Corner of coursed, random ashlar with anchor irons; window with jack arch

WA-103 Limestone in coursed ashlar with molding course and framed, recessed panels, water-damage weathering

WA-104 Siena marble veneer on staircase soffit, molding and pilaster

WA-105 Split-faced coursed ashlar granite wall with dentil cornice and arched windows: Florentine (left and center), segmental (right), with jack-arch entries below

STONE WALLS

WA-106 Inside-corner turret in coursed rubble with dimension-stone quoins on outside corners and around window

WA-107 Banded marble in alternating polychrome ashlar courses with relieving arch

WA-108 Random rubble of cobbles with rusticated dimension-brownstone quoins, belt course, and voussoirs around arch window

WA-109 Granite in random ashlar with corbelled jetty, dimension-stone window quoins

STONE WALLS

WA-110 Entry wall with flagstones in staggered shelf courses

WA-111 Shale fieldstone in coursed roughly squared rubble and herringbone pattern

WA-112 Rusticated running bond with hand-tooled finish; sand-finish keystone; crossettes; carved ornamented belt course

WA-113 Weathered sand-finish limestone in running bond, with cartouche keystone in stepped arch

STONE WALLS

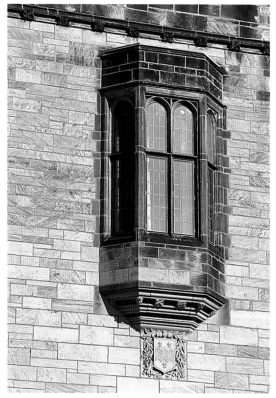

WA-114 Partially cleaned Indiana Birmingham buff limestone, sawn veneer, in random ashlar with oriel

WA-115 Weathered limestone in coursed ashlar with dentil and modillion cornice; carved ornament on columns and window frames

WA-116 Sawn fossil-stone in coursed ashlar with raised voussoirs; engaged balustrade with bead base molding above belt course

WA-117 Rock-face brownstone in random ashlar; sand-finished belt course, trefoil carved lintel

WA-118 Limestone in running bond with cornice; upper story with carved spandrels; varied window openings

WA-119 Sand-finish limestone veneer with Art Deco bas-relief cartouche and molding

STONE WALLS

WA-120 Alternating polychrome bands of marble veneer in stack and running bonds with Moorish blind arches with recessed windows

WA-121 Staircase wall in coursed ashlar with Gothic blind arches and engaged columns

WA-122 Staircase wall in mosaic-bond rubble with niches and stone coping

STONE WALLS

WA-123 Gable-end wall in random ashlar; block modillion cornice; quoins around arched windows; corbelled window sill (left)

WA-124 Battered-wall base in coursed roughly squared ashlar

WA-125 Granite in running bond with rustic accents; neo-Corinthian pilasters in stack bond flanking entry

STONE WALLS

WA-126 Sawn-fossil-stone wall and staircase in coursed ashlar

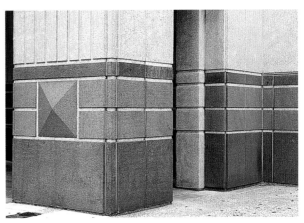

WA-127 Corner detail of polychrome banded granite veneer with gem-cut decorative block

WA-128 Rock-face granite doorway lintel with contrasting sawn-granite panels in running bond with wide V-shaped joints

WA-129 Inside and outside corners of slate roof and cladding, modern commercial building

WA-130 Inside and outside corners of end-matched travertine veneer on walls and post, modern commercial building

STONE WALLS

WA-131 Outside corner of granite veneer with raked joints; belt courses at window and jetty, modern commercial building

WA-132 Corner of rusticated running bond with reveal; sand-finish pilaster strips in stack bond on entry, modern commercial building

WA-133 Corner of split-face granite in shelf, running bond with metal banding, modern commercial building

WA-134 Inside corner of honed-granite veneer in stack bond with grouted joints and window reveal, modern commercial building

WA-135 Limestone-veneer panels framed by contrasting stack-and-running-bond courses, modern commercial building

WA-136 Banded polished-granite-veneer spandrels alternating with honed granite and ribbon windows, modern commercial building

WA-137 Honed-granite veneer in stack bond with raised pattern around windows, modern commercial building

STONE WALLS

WA-138 Granite veneer with contrasting granite window inserts surmounted by space frame, modern commercial building

WA-139 Stone in running bond with projecting window sills and rock-faced decorative blocks, modern commercial building

WA-140 Granite with tinted mortar, fixed windows, modern commercial building

WA-141 Polished granite veneer with flush-mounted fixed windows in polychrome curtain wall, modern commercial building

STONE WALLS

WA-142 Sandstone coursed-ashlar frame with stack-bond inset, flush marble-veneer base, modern commercial building

WA-143 Red sandstone with natural cleft face, coursed ashlar with sand-finish belt courses above door and black granite base, modern commercial building

WA-144 Granite, with honed and gem-cut blocks in running bond, modern commercial building

WA-145 Polished veneer in polychrome bands with pilaster strips, modern commercial building

WA-146 Honed granite in stack bond with polychrome bands, modern apartment house

WA-147 Contrasting sand-finished brownstone panels, modern commercial building

WA-148 Polychrome stone-veneer collage of polished and honed granites, modern commercial building

STONE WALLS

WALLS

WA-149 Left: Flemish-bond inset panel and frame with raised horizontal panel in basket-weave and rowlock bonds; right: white glazed brick on banded pilaster in running bond

WA-150 Rusticated brick in Flemish bond, shelf angle, with curved corner above granite rock-face belt course and honed base

WA-151 Erratic Flemish bond with a sloping course and rowlock-course coping

WA-152 Custom-sculpted and glazed brick, modern residential courtyard

BRICK WALLS

WA-153 Common bond, seventh-course header, in garden wall with repairs

WA-154 Raised shaped decorative panel in English bond, late 18th-c. building

WA-155 Roman brick with projecting soldier course and elliptical arch with stone corbels, ancient Roman wall

WA-156 Basket-weave borders around running-bond; concrete capstone, garden wall

WA-157 Notched garden wall in Flemish bond with rowlock-course coping

WA-158 Roman bricks with soldier course and shaped bricks forming crenel, ancient parapet wall

Photo: Austin, Patterson, Disston

WA-159 Ancient Roman brick running-bond wall with stone quoins, banding course, and bead molding

WA-160 Ancient Roman wall with exposed rubble, running and diagonal bonds

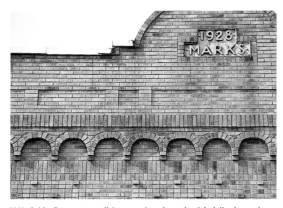

WA-161 Parapet wall in running bond with blind semi-circular arches and corbels below soldier course

WA-162 Roman brick with pilaster, ancient wall

WA-163 Ancient Roman brick wall with structural dog-tooth course exposed by weathering of brick facing layer

WA-164 Medieval arcade under relieving arch in gauged brick with chevron-decorated extrados and recessed spandrels

WA-165 Inside corner of Flemish-bond wall with ogee water-table course

WA-166 Multiple bonds. Left to right: Flemish bond; rowlock and header frame; basket-weave

WA-167 Roman brick screen, Tuscan farm wall

WA-168 Radial brick in running bond on curved wall

WA-169 Detail of gauged-brick arch surrounded by running bond

WA-170 Multiple bonds in custom-sized brick. Top and right: raised header courses; center: patterns in stacked stretchers, soldier, and headers

WA-171 Custom design: multiple geometric patterns in multiple bonds

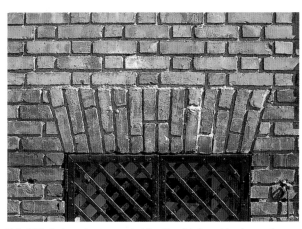

WA-172 Jack arch surrounded by Flemish bond in alternating colors

WA-173 Jack-arch window and dog-tooth course of contrasting brick in English bond wall with recessed panel

WA-174 Star anchor iron in running-bond brick wall with relieving arch

WA-175 Weathered brick in running bond on rough split-faced foundation and bricked-in arch windows with stone sills, alley wall

WA-176 Painted rock-face brick with dentil molding, pilasters, and double window under arch in recessed panel with cartouche

WA-177 Modern variation of Roman brick in running bond with tinted mortar and soldier base course; louvered shutters on door and window

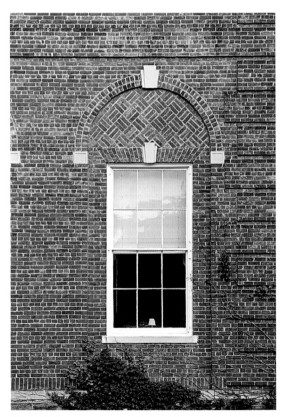

WA-178 Common bond with fourth-course header, blind arch of diagonal basket-weave over window, and raised quoin corners

WA-179 Mottled effect in polychrome toned brick, modern residential building

WA-180 Brick panels in running bond articulated by joints and soldier courses; soldier courses top and bottom of windows, modern commercial building

WA-181 Flemish bond on curved entry with brick steps and window sill; variation of dog's tooth on corner (far left)

WA-182 Common bond with sixth-course headers; recessed spandrels with checker pattern; soldier course above windows

BRICK WALLS

WA-183 Rusticated-brick corner; window with rowlock sill, and raised stacked bond imitating shutters, modern apartment house

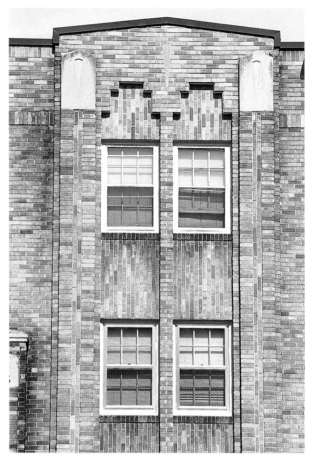

WA-184 Idiosyncratic collection of stacked bond and horizontal and vertical running bonds on pilasters and spandrels; rowlock window sills

WA-185 Semicircular arches in blind arcade on brick wall with terracotta frieze above raised panel, Beaux-Arts commercial building

WA-186 Radial brick corner with banding in contrasting colors and masonry; segmental-arch windows, modern commercial building

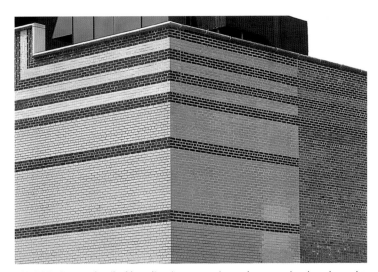

WA-187 Corner detail of banding in contrasting colors; running bond, modern commercial building

WA-188 Contrasting brick banding and pilasters; gauged-brick semicircular arches on upper windows, 19th-c. apartment house

BRICK WALLS

WA-189 Romanesque-style decorative brickwork with
ornate corbel on corner below parapet roof

WA-190 Curved corner banded with courses of stretcher
bricks and sculpted brick or architectural terracotta

WA-191 Corner detail of bands of running bond,
rowlock and soldier courses in contrasting colors, modern
commercial building

WA-192 Corner detail of brick and molded decorative
brick or terracotta, 19th-c. apartment house

WA-193 Corner detail of brick with banding in contrasting colors and vertical expansion/sealant joints, modern commercial building

WA-194 Corner detail of custom bond with dog-tooth banding and diaper pattern of projecting stretchers, modern apartment house

WA-195 Corner detail of common bond, sixth-course header, with dog's-tooth corner

WA-196 Corner detail of Romanesque-style brick building with stone banding, parapet roof with crenellation

WA-197 Brick window-wall with recessed spandrels, brownstone window trim and quoins

WA-198 Corner detail of decorative brickwork: diaper-patterned brickwork in contrasting colors with roundels and vertical stripes suggesting fluted pilasters

WA-199 Gauged-brick segmental window arch with stone keystone under decorative brickwork of multi-colored English cross bond

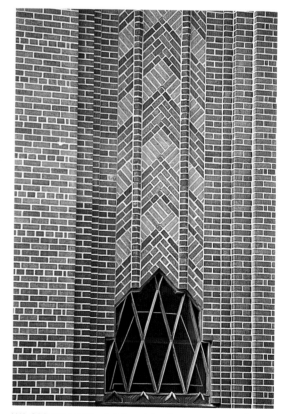

WA-200 Decorative brickwork in chevron pattern of running and stacked bonds; header rows framing grate in recessed panel

WA-201 Pilasters in running bond with variation of dog's-tooth edge; inset panel of decorative brickwork in herringbone pattern with projecting bricks

WA-202 Bands of decorative brickwork: running bond alternating with projecting soldier rows; rowlock and soldiers around roundel, modern commercial building

WA-203 Bands of decorative brickwork. Top to bottom: chevron, horizontal banding, diaper-work

WA-204 Bands of decorative brickwork. Left to right: terracotta arch, stacked header rows, basket-weave, stacked header rows, English bond

WA-205 Brick in stack bond with subtle soldier-course banding, modern apartment house

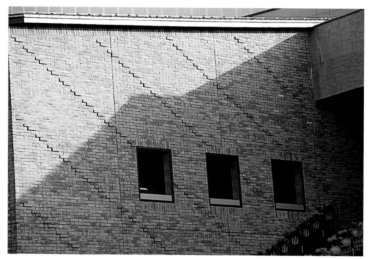

WA-206 Brick in random tones with projecting diagonal pattern and soldier courses above square windows, modern commercial building

WA-207 Decorative brickwork. Left to right: square brick or tile in diagonal pattern with brick window ornament; projecting ornament over stacked bond pilasters, 19th-c. French apartment house

BRICK WALLS

WA-208 Weathered cast-in-place concrete with smooth finish; metal and glass upper story, modern house

WA-209 Board-formed concrete with textured finish from wood formwork, residential courtyard

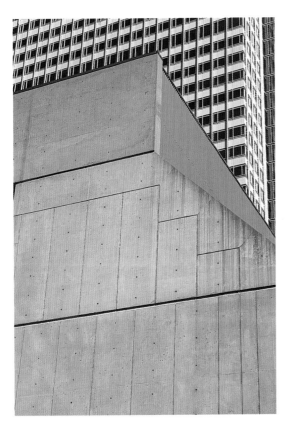

WA-210 Cast concrete with smooth finish, articulated formwork panels, and horizontal expansion joints

WA-211 Corner detail of cast concrete with banding and interlocking panels, modern commercial building

WA-212 Polychrome banded cast concrete, modern commercial building

WA-213 Board-formed concrete with textured finish from wood formwork

WA-214 Concrete board siding cast with a wood board-and-batten pattern

WA-215 Cast concrete, shower room

Photo: Austin, Patterson, Disston

WA-216 Concrete projecting window, modern house

WA-217 Cast coarse-aggregate concrete, bush-hammered, with board-formed slab edge

WA-218 Manufactured stone in rubble wall, residential wall

WA-219 Pre-cast textured concrete with chevron and diaper patterns

WA-220 Pre-cast coarse-aggregate concrete, modern commercial building

WA-221 Weathered handmade concrete block with mortar in irregular running bond on house

WA-222 Inside corner of mortared structural-block walls in running bond

WA-223 Concrete-block dry wall in irregular running bond, industrial wall

WA-224 Stucco finish applied in rectangular concrete framework imitating masonry in running bond

WA-225 Interior and exterior corners of split-face concrete walls with banding and smooth-faced and contrasting color block, modern commercial building

WA-226 Split-face concrete block in running bond with pink banding, modern commercial building

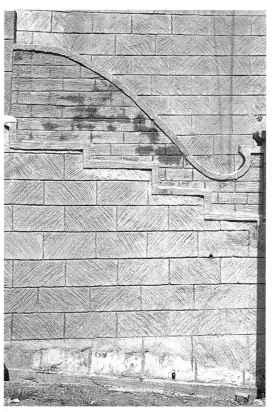

WA-227 Carved concrete block textured to resemble sawn stone in running bond with stepped band under curved guard wall

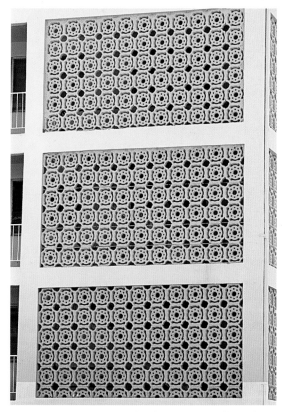

WA-228 Custom concrete blocks in screen wall, residential entryway

WA-229 Custom concrete blocks with screen wall (top), residential entryway

WA-230 Stucco with dimension-stone window and corner quoins and natural stone insets in serpentine design; louvered shutters, house

WA-231 Detail of arched opening with impost-like molding, stucco over adobe, American Southwestern mission

WA-232 Flared, rounded corner of smoothed painted stucco imitating a detail of traditional American Southwestern adobe house

WA-233 Smoothed and whitewashed mud plaster over adobe brick on a base of fieldstone, courtyard wall

STUCCO & CONCRETE WALLS

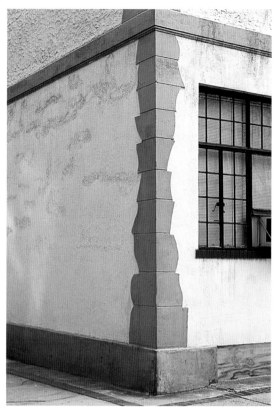

WA-234 Smooth stucco quoins and belt course on textured stucco building

WA-235 Undulating stucco finish on gable-end wall, industrial building

WA-236 Colored rough-troweled finish on stucco with smooth stucco band forming jetty, Italian-villa–style modern commercial building

WA-237 Inscribed design in grouted blocks running along jetty, modern commercial building

WA-238 Knocked-down skip-troweled stucco finish on beach house

WA-239 Textured and inscribed stucco, foliated and pictorial designs mixed with imitation split-face stone in running bond

WA-240 Cast concrete walls imitating stack bond, base course decorated with imprints of children's hands, urban public space

WA-241 Stucco over random ashlar stone

WA-242 Weathered undulating smooth stucco on painted wall with a variety of windows, urban house

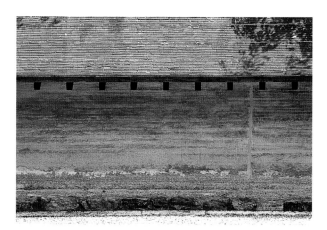

WA-243 Mud wall with layers of tinted mud stucco, courtyard wall

WA-244 Whitewashed undulating smooth stucco wall with shuttered windows, apartment house

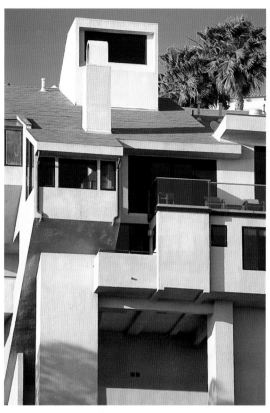

WA-245 Painted smooth stucco, modern house

WA-246 Colored stucco with knocked-down skip-trowel finish on wall; double hung windows, Italian-villa–style modern apartment house

WA-247 Colored smooth stucco supergraphic with stucco quoins in lower section, modern apartment house

WA-248 Weathered colored smooth stucco; pilasters and arched windows

WA-249 Large-aggregate stucco with cobbles and quoins on weathered gable-end wall, farm building

WA-250 Weathered colored smooth stucco surrounding oval window with grille and ornate frame; hipped tile roof

Photo: Meredith Barchat

WA-251 Painted stucco textures on gable-end wall

Photo: Meredith Barchat

WA-252 Weathered stucco wall surrounding balcony with stucco-covered pillars

WA-253 Weathered tinted mud stucco revealing rammed mud wall

WA-254 Weathered painted plaster revealing structural stone and wood cladding

WA-255 Weathered colored smooth stucco on courtyard wall with balcony

WA-256 Weathered colored stucco revealing timber lintel, scratch coat and structural stone, and Roman brick

WA-257 Weathered colored stucco, Italianate building

WA-258 Walls of plastered interior apartment walls exposed by demolition

WA-259 Weathered whitewashed mud-stucco over exposed adobe brick courtyard wall, American Southwestern mission

WA-260 Weathered stucco exposing structural brick and stone. Original plasterwork included faux-stone quoins and blocks in running bond

WA-261 Weathered stucco wall with pilaster

WA-262 Weathered whitewashed mud-stucco with invasive tropical vegetation on garden wall

WA-263 Weathered stucco with concrete patches, graffiti, and exposed structural brick and stone

WA-264 Courtyard wall. Top to bottom: rowlock and header brick coping; cast concrete (left); running-bond brick pilaster; roughly squared fieldstone base

WA-265 Brick-and-fieldstone lamppost at driveway entry, Arts and Crafts residence

WA-266 Courtyard wall. Top to bottom: cast-concrete coping; saw-tooth brick course; light-colored stone, herringbone-bond brick in concrete frame; painted brick; stone base

WA-267 Coursed ashlar stone panel in brick frame, garden wall

WA-268 Single courses of slate alternating with double courses of brick in running bond, garden wall

WA-269 Random-bond brick with roughly squared fieldstone

WA-270 Vertical planks of weathered cedar shaped to fit profile of fieldstone base

WA-271 Colored stucco wall with fossil-stone coping and base

WA-272 Boulders and large cobbles randomly interspersed with custom-bond brick, openings filled with grillework or screen blocks, battered garden wall

MIXED MATERIALS

WA-273 Diamond-shaped panels on half-timbered and pegged construction

WA-274 Stucco and wood-planked infill; timber-frame construction; traditional Japanese wood lattice window

WA-275 Stucco infill; post-and-beam wall with decorative metal tie-irons at intersections of posts and beams, bell-shaped sliding shutter

WA-276 Half-timber construction with corbels under jetty; leaded windows, and console supports under oriel, 16th- or 17th-c. English house

WA-277 Half-timbering with brick infill (top) and stucco (bottom), 17th-c. French house

MIXED MATERIALS

WA-278 Decorative half-timbered facade with concrete infill and copper "timbers," 20th-c. residential building

WA-279 Post-and-beam construction with stucco and wood-plank infill; partially dressed timber post, traditional Japanese building

WA-280 Half-timbering; fieldstone under jetty, 16th- or 17th-c. English house

WA-281 Timber frame with infill of undulating stucco and framed planks, traditional Japanese building

WA-282 Half-timber with brick infill; fieldstone first story, 16th- or 17th-c. English house

WA-283 Half-timber with stucco infill, 15th- or 16th-c. French house

WA-284 Half-timber with brick infill, 15th- or 16th-c. French house

WA-285 Decorative half-timbered facade with flat wood "timbers," brick infill, and bay windows, 20th-c. house

MIXED MATERIALS

WA-286 Ancient arcade. Top to bottom: roughly squared stone; diaper brickwork; courses of stone and Roman brick, weathered tile with substructure, brick-and-stone arches; coursed-ashlar stone

WA-287 Banded brick-and-stone arches with carved ornament in keystones and spandrels

WA-288 Uncoursed rubble wall with brick-framed windows and brick belt courses; cambered arch window with trompe l'oeil grille and shutters

WA-289 Coursed ashlar on inside-corner turret with corbelled jetty and adjacent upper story; remaining walls of brick

MIXED MATERIALS

WA-290 Rusticated stone blocks in running bond, surrounded by brick; egg-and-dart pilaster cap and molding, with relief ornament band between stories

WA-291 Half-timber upper story with brick infill and stucco lower story with stone quoins

WA-292 Brick with stone quoins between spandrels with geometric tile patterns

WA-293 Black granite base with metal-and-glass curtain wall, modern commercial building

WA-294 Banded running-bond brickwork on upper stories with supergraphic running repeat in cast concrete or stone, modern commercial building

WA-295 Brick in running-bond bands with stone or pre-cast concrete, modern commercial building

WA-296 Brick, metal mesh, and stone, modern commercial building

MIXED MATERIALS

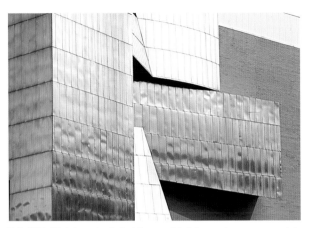

WA-297 Stainless steel cladding and brick, modern commercial building

WA-298 Metal-framed glass panels with colored and patinated metal, modern commercial building

WA-299 Split-face sandstone veneer next to colored-glass or plexiglass-clad wing, modern commercial building

WA-300 Split-face sandstone with glass block and tile (top left), modern commercial building

WA-301 Glass and stone curtain walls, modern commercial building

WA-302 Top to bottom: batten-seam metal cladding; cast concrete or stone; metal shingles; metal-framed glass, modern commercial building

WA-303 Concrete building with metal trim

WA-304 Stone veneer and brick wing with stone-veneer quoins, modern commercial building

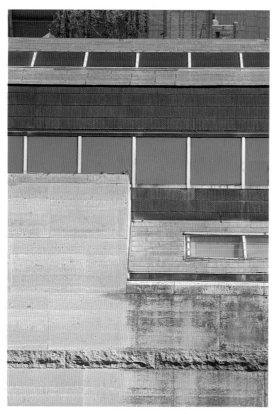

WA-305 Top to bottom: patinated corrugated metal cladding; coursed ashlar sandstone with rock-face belt course, modern commercial building

MIXED MATERIALS

WA-306 Glass-block tower with stepped cast concrete at base next to cast-concrete Art Deco–style modern residential building

WA-307 Stone-veneer lower story and tile-clad upper stories, modern commercial building

WA-308 Glass, stone, and brick modern commercial building

WA-309 Interior metal cladding with banded brick below, modern industrial building

FACADES

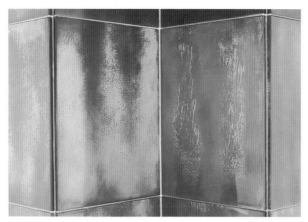

FA-1 Corner detail of clear-coated verdigris cladding, with grouted seams

FA-2 Steel or aluminum wall standing-seam cladding, modern commercial building

FA-3 Weathered stamped-tin sheathing in faux stone pattern

FA-4 Painted corrugated metal screen wall with elliptical cutouts, urban park

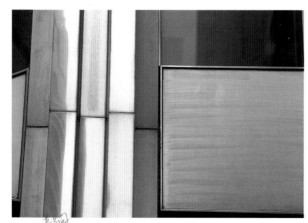

FA-5 Bronze over stainless steel spandrel panel with a raised edge and adjoining window (top right)

FA-6 Weathered flat metal panels with visible fasteners, probably lapped, exterior wall of industrial building

FA-7 Metal-clad modern house. Top: adjacent vertical strips; strip window; bottom: flush panels (left); contrasting metal entry (right)

FA-8 Flush curved mirror-finished stainless steel cladding, modern commercial building

FA-9 Brushed stainless steel cladding with stamped ornamental moldings and exposed fasteners, American diner

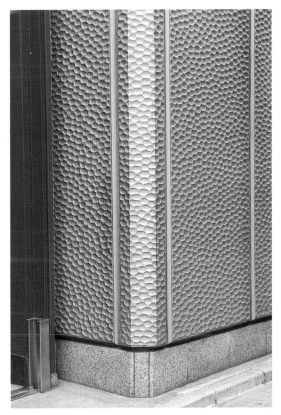

FA-10 Vertical cladding with hammered finish

FA-11 Weathered and naturally patinated pier with prominent fasteners, ancient Japanese entry

FA-12 Corrugated metal patinated shingles surrounding strip windows and skylights

FA-13 Copper cladding, modern commercial building

FA-14 Curtain wall; spandrel panels with dimensional geometric pattern, modern commercial building

FA-15 Flush cast-bronze cladding, entry of modern institutional building

FA-16 Galvanized metal cladding in running-bond pattern

FA-17 Copper panels, possibly with standing vertical seams, lapped horizontally

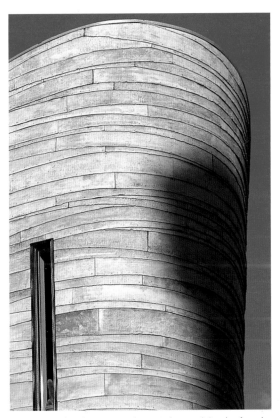

FA-18 Metal strips wrapped around a semicircular facade with irregular laps and visible fasteners

FA-19 Possibly galvanized steel, batten-seam vertical panels
els 镀锌

FA-20 Corrugated galvanized steel panels with visible fasteners, modern commercial building

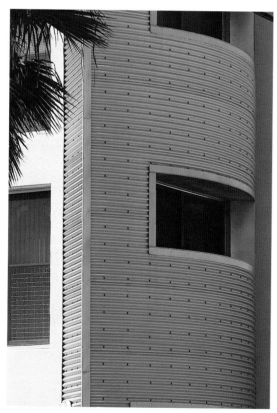

FA-21 Painted curved corrugated metal panels with visible fasteners and strip windows, modern residential building

FA-22 Flush galvanized panels, modern commercial building

FA-23 Weathered panelized wall system with stamped diamond pattern, modern apartment house

FA-24 Painted and patinated metal panels with lapped seams, modern commercial building

FA-25 Reinforced concrete frame with black acid-etched stainless steel panels and windows, modern institutional building

FACADES

FA-26 Stainless steel shingle cladding with lapped seams, modern institutional building

FA-27 Ovoid projection on facade made of custom fabricated metal panels, modern commercial building

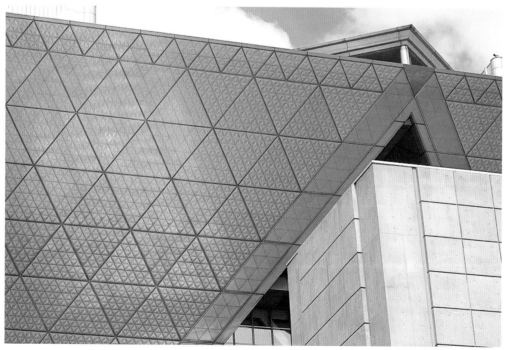

FA-28 Stamped metal panels in a triangular pattern on space frame, entry to modern commercial building

FA-29 Fully glazed curved curtain walls with mirror glass

FA-30 Banded curtain wall, alternating mirror glass and solid spandrel panels

Photo: Guy Gurney

FA-31 Banded curtain wall, alternating mirror glass spandrels and windows

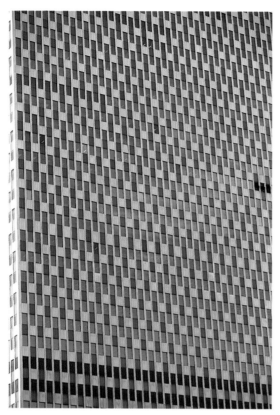

FA-32 Cladding system of staggered spandrel elements, probably pre-cast concrete and glass

FA-33 Curtain wall around a stair tower with glass panels secured at corners by a bracket system and seams sealed with silicone

FA-34 Banded curtain wall, alternating mirror glass and solid spandrel panels

FA-35 Glass-block curtain wall with rounded corner

CURTAIN WALLS

FA-36 Left to right: fully glazed; alternating solid spandrel panels and glazing; curtain-wall system with column covers and glazed units

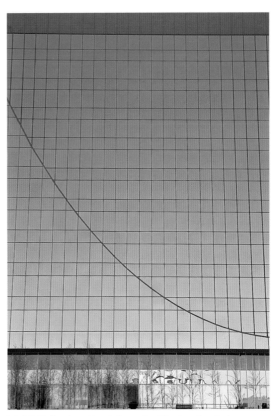

FA-37 Fully glazed curtain wall with glass inset above curve; recessed mirror glass at bottom reflects trees in courtyard

FA-38 Fully glazed curtain wall, shading louvers visible at lower level. Projections may be structural bracket system or ornamental

FA-39 Panelized cladding system with fully glazed curtain wall of light spectrum-producing glass or plastic enclosing elevator shaft

CURTAIN WALLS

FA-40 Fully glazed curtain wall of bronze mirror glass with horizontal mullions emphasized

FA-41 Fully glazed curtain wall, windows with metal frames

FA-42 Photovoltaic-panel cladding, modern commercial building

Photo: Austin, Patterson, Disston

FA-43 New Alaskan yellow cedar shakes in common coursing, corner detail

FA-44 Weathered sawn shingles in fish-scale pattern on ogee roof

FA-45 Clapboard and sawn siding in fish-scale pattern with corner board, flat applied trim, and lunette window

FA-46 Painted shakes in staggered course

FA-47 Painted sawn shingles in fish-scale pattern, gable detail

FA-48 Painted sawn shingles in fish-scale pattern on shed dormer

FA-49 Weathered Alaskan yellow cedar shakes in common coursing and segmental arch window, corner and roof detail

FA-50 Cut shingles on gable. Top: wave pattern around bull's-eye window; bottom: fish-scale pattern

FA-51 Left: shakes in common coursing with scalloped cut shingles; right: cut shingles, alternating fish-scale and scalloped patterns; shake border

FA-52 New Alaskan yellow cedar shakes in common coursing, eyebrow window; gambrel roof

SHINGLES

FA-53 Bituminous shingles in diamond pattern (top), staggered course (bottom)

FA-54 Bituminous shingles in staggered course below bracketed cornice

FA-55 Bituminous shingles in faux ashlar stone pattern

FA-56 Weathered bituminous shingles in faux brick pattern, exposed wood cladding

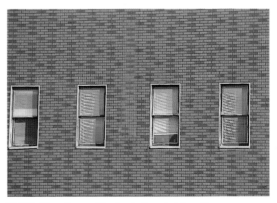

FA-57 Bituminous shingles in multicolored hexagonal pattern

FA-58 Bituminous shingles in faux brick pattern

SHINGLES

FA-59 Brick facade with polychrome glazed ornamental details: bracket cornice, cartouches, garlands, ancon, and rope molding around semicircular windows

FA-60 Ornate banded stone-finish architectural terracotta facade with pilasters

FA-61 Polychrome architectural terracotta facade with arabesque ornament

Photo: Duane Langenwalter

FA-62 Glazed polychrome relief tiles with dragon design on exterior wall

FA-63 Plain masonry facade with architectural terracotta ornament

FA-64 Brick facade with polychrome terracotta ornament

FA-65 Mosaic entablature with arabesque ornament and cartouche

FA-66 Glazed tiles with Middle Eastern pattern and tile-trimmed windows, courtyard wall

FA-67 Marble mosaic wall adjacent to a marble pilaster

FA-68 Textured matte tiles with glass-block windows, entry of modern house

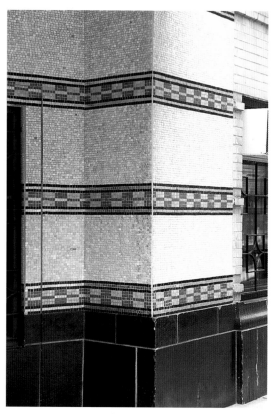

FA-69 Mosaic with horizontal bands of tiles in geometric pattern, entry of modern apartment house

FA-70 Glazed patterned tiles around square windows with metal grille and wood shutter and ogee windows with grille, Turkey

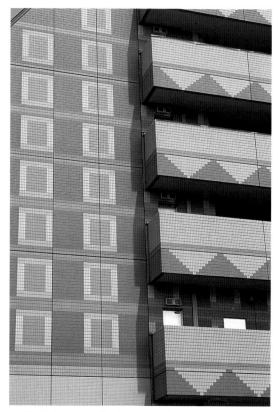

FA-71 Polychrome tiles in geometric patterns on walls and balconies of modern apartment house

FA-72 Traditional bright colors painted on stucco walls, door, and shutters, Central America

FA-73 Traditional red painted wood-infill post-and-beam facade and paneled door, Japanese entry gate

FA-74 Brick wall with painted geometric design and painted metal sculptural elements on store exterior

Photo: Meredith Barchat

FA-75 Trabeated cast-iron facade painted in nontraditional colors

FA-76 Painted textured stucco with contrasting color around window, contemporary house

FA-77 Tudor-arch doorway and adjacent oriel painted with exterior gloss colors, 19th-c. storefront

FA-78 Stucco-covered adobe painted with floral and ornamental bands on facade with window and exposed lintel, 18th-c. American Southwestern mission

PAINTED WALLS

FA-79 Polychrome house with octagonal turret, steep gable dormer, prominent bargeboards, fish-scale cut siding, and modillion cornice, 19th-c.

FA-80 Octagonal turret on contemporary polychrome house, modillion cornice, repeated ornament, and ornamental shutters around windows

FA-81 Painted garage with shingles on gable end, vertical tongue-and-groove siding and door

PAINTED WALLS

FA-82 Weathered trompe l'oeil quoins and stone detail on Tuscan wall

FA-83 Weathered trompe l'oeil moldings and pediment around shuttered windows on Tuscan wall

FA-84 Courtyard wall of painted stone and concrete block with scribed lines simulating masonry, Indonesia

FA-85 Courtyard wall and steps: weathered pilasters with painted flutes and ornament, Indonesia

FA-86 Decorative painting of foliated ornament around rusticated arch and window on stucco Tuscan wall

FA-87 Sgraffito depicting pilasters, enriched archivolts, classical moldings, reticulated band with paterae on wall, Italy

PAINTED WALLS

FA-88 Painted geometric pattern on brick facade of industrial building (paint manufacturer)

FA-89 Multicolored painted plywood cladding on building under renovation

FA-90 Trompe l'oeil clouds and sky on brick facade with dog-tooth courses

FA-91 Trompe l'oeil stucco simulating adjacent masonry on belfry, dome with chamfered corners, 19th-c. mission

FA-92 Weathered painted stucco over exposed brick with half-timber gable above

FA-93 Painted stucco facades, Italian riverfront buildings

FA-94 Weathered painted clapboard facade

FA-95 Weathered painted stucco over brick

FA-96 Painted advertisement on stucco wall, France

FA-97 Weathered painted advertisement on weathered urban brick wall

FA-98 Peeling paint on poured-in-place concrete frame with scored simulated masonry joints

FA-99 Peeling paint on brick garden wall with stone base

FA-100 Weathered painted vertical board-and-batten wall and adjacent masonry structure

FA-101 Weathered painted clapboard and siding with diagonal board framed door

FA-102 Sign painted in graffiti style on brick and corrugated metal urban wall

FA-103 Painted advertisement on brick facade

Photo: Duane Langenwalter

FA-104 Painted sign on painted tongue-and-groove facade

FA-105 Painted sign on brick facade with loading door

FA-106 Painted sign on blank brick facade

FA-107 Graffiti painted on brick pier between garage doors

FA-108 Detail of polychrome compound-arch portal in Gothic style, with three jamb shafts

FA-109 Stair tower with engaged columns and spiral balustrade

FA-110 Brick facade with traditional stone carving and grotesque figures, Indonesian temple

FA-111 Diamond-patterned brick facade with window arcade, framed by a rusticated corner pilaster and cornice

FA-112 Molded cornices and window surrounds with running ornament on multistory masonry facade

FA-113 Balconies over portal, broken pediment, and ornate details on multistory masonry facade

FA-114 Ornate balconies of carved and pierced wood on multistory facade, India

Photo: Meredith Barchat

FA-115 Stucco facade with older arches embedded in the wall adjacent to modern windows

FA-116 Art Deco facade, highly polished stone cladding with geometric ornament below white glazed brick

FA-117 Neo-Gothic ornamental features with ornamental spandrels in brick facade

FA-118 Brick facade with stone or cast rams-head-and-snake ornaments and running geometric ornament in spandrel bands

FACADE ORNAMENT

FA-119 Brick facade with decorative masonry frieze of sculpted spandrels between windows

FA-120 Stone facade with relief foliated arabesque ornament on spandrels

FA-121 Brick facade with rusticated and heavy embellishment in brownstone or terracotta

FA-122 Facade clad in heavily embellished relief panels

FA-123 Portal with coupled engaged columns and balcony heavily ornamented and embellished with cartouches, 18th-c. English country house

FA-124 Polychrome facade with low relief ornament in stucco and cast concrete, Art Deco hotel

FA-125 Curtain-wall system of multicolored panels, supergraphic, modern commercial building

FA-126 Curving glass curtain wall above stone-veneer facade with expressed piers and keyhole window surrounds, modern commercial building

FA-127 Trabeated facade finished in colors suggesting post-and-lintel construction, modern mixed-use building

FACADE ORNAMENT

FA-128 Curtain wall with geometric design in clear and opaque glass spandrels and column covers with raised edges and mullions

FA-129 Curtain-wall panels in multiple bands with ventilation grilles incorporated in projecting ornamental pyramid and circle-in-square motifs

FA-130 Facade of simple punched windows, curvilinear balconies, and large-scale open grid, modern apartment house

FA-131 Trabeated facade with multicolored infill and spandrel panels, modern commercial building

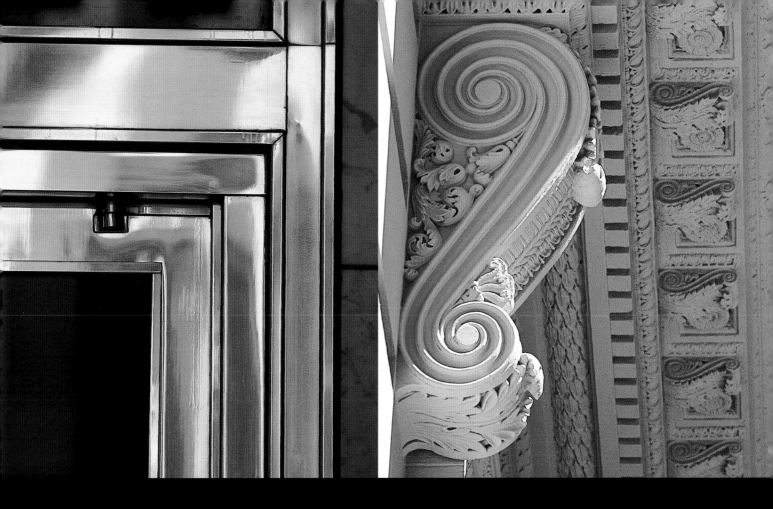

ORNAMENT & MOLDING

OM-1 Bands. Top to bottom: triangles and rosettes; square inset panels with star and rosette; gilded foliated motif, vertical reeding, dart motif

OM-2 Cast bronze octagonal coffer with central rosette surrounded by shell-motif molding

OM-3 Cast bronze frieze based on classical entablature: Pegasus figures ("metopes") alternating with "torch" ornaments ("triglyphs")

OM-4 Bands. Top to bottom: stylized Vitruvian scroll with shell antefix; vertical corrugated pattern; rope molding, and foliated ovolo molding with pattern reversed at center

OM-5 Volute on bronze scrolled pediment. Molding, top to bottom: corona with band ornament; egg-and-dart ovolo; tongue-and-dart cyma reversa

OM-6 Bronze panels with vertical reeding below geometric profile with floral medallions and banded geometric ornamented frame

OM-7 Detail of bronze scrolled pediment with anthemion finials

OM-8 Nickel-silver-plated bronze or cast stainless steel spandrel panels with seahorse ornament

OM-9 Carved wood ancon with mascaron

OM-10 Antic bracket in the form of a dragon

OM-11 Brackets: square panel surrounded by a garland
with a lion's-head antic in front of a scroll

OM-12 Console with acanthus leaves

OM-13 Foliated ornament over doorway flanked by zig-zag (top) and dentilated (bottom) bands

OM-14 Corner detail of plain tablets with festoons and drapery ornament

OM-15 Console with acanthus leaves, flanked by festoons

OM-16 Antic ornament, Indonesia

OM-17 Sculptural vignette set in a plain plastered corner

OM-18 Antic corner ornament, Indonesia

OM-19 Ornament, griffin holding a book

Photo: Duane Langenwalter

OM-20 Polychrome relief carving, monkeys in a tree, Japan

OM-21 Lion gargoyle

ARCHITECTURAL ORNAMENT

OM-22 Cartouche with building date

OM-23 Cartouche with regimental arms surrounded by flags, cannons, drums, and fife

OM-24 Cartouche with building number above guttae, with festoon and center antic

OM-25 Tympanum with foliated ornament, concave oval cartouche with gilded building number

OM-26 Consoles flanking a date stone with bird ornament in relief

OM-27 Convex oval cartouche with building number over a plain lintel with a festoon

ARCHITECTURAL ORNAMENT

OM-28 Weathered stone tablet with Latin inscription

OM-29 Sandstone cartouche in square panel with a mascaron inside a sunburst

OM-30 Cartouche with Arabic inscription, surrounded by foliated ornament

OM-31 Large cartouche surmounted by a crown, with molded frame with crossettes, surrounded by smaller cartouches of similar design

OM-32 Three cartouches over an entryway, the center one flanked by two cherubs

OM-33 Ornamental band with serpentine motif and rosette in an octagonal frame

OM-34 Ornamental band with rosettes in a Greek-key motif, over egg-and-dart molding

OM-35 Ornamental band with Vitruvian scroll below blind balustrade

OM-36 Foliated ornament and open book with Hebrew inscription on base course of a corbel under an oriel

OM-37 Polychrome ornamental bands: wide central band with a circle motif, flanked by thin bands with linear patterns; foliated band on the bottom

OM-38 Ornamental band with interlocking palm motif below the coping of a garden wall

OM-39 Shaft on a mascaron bracket. At left, foliated sculptural panel with a cherub

OM-40 Portal with sculpted spandrel, ancon keystone below Doric-style entablature with sculpted metopes and triglyphs

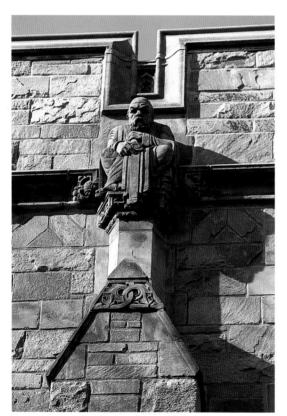

OM-41 Figurative finial on a wall buttress

OM-42 Anta with relief winged mythological figure holding palm fronds below cornice with egg-and-dart ovolo molding and an alternating dentil and modillion band

Photo: The Preservation Society of Newport County

OM-43 Niche covered by a baldachin on Gothic-style entry

OM-44 Stepped and foliated ornamental pattern with antic figure on temple entry, Bali

OM-45 Cartouche surmounted by antic. Enriched molding, top to bottom: foliated cyma reversa; foliated cyma recta; egg-and-dart ovolo; tongue-and-dart; bead-and-reel

OM-46 Mascarons and botanical ornaments on a concave molding on an archivolt

OM-47 Foliated shaft with Mesoamerican-style mascaron

OM-48 Foliated ornament with acanthus leaves on weathered stone door surround

OM-49 Gilded ornament: large medallions, foliated band, bracket with a mascaron, and central finial

OM-50 Carved stone mascaron keystone

OM-51 Stone relief frieze over entry: bull's-eye window framed by draped figures, scroll motifs, and Composite capitals on flat pilasters

OM-52 Arch with sculpted spandrel. Entablature with frieze and festoons between consoles terminating in guttae below molding

OM-53 Stylized broken scrolled pediment over a plain cornice and inscribed architrave

OM-54 Door surround with rosettes; cavetto cornice with anthemion motif and antefix at corner; pier capped by anthemion

OM-55 Crossette surround with Greek-key motif, terminated with three guttae; framed lozenge design in spandrel panel

OM-56 Left: scrolled archivolt terminating at a foliated impost; right: banding with guilloche pattern

ARCHITECTURAL ORNAMENT

OM-57 Greek-key band with square floral element; jamb molding with rosettes framed by ornamented ovolo molding

OM-58 Corner detail of foliated ornament, shield device, and grotesque

OM-59 Antefixes on cornice over a portal, the center one a mascaron

OM-60 Foliated arabesque frieze with central lion's head over an arcade

OM-61 Top to bottom: cartouche over a niche; alternating ornamental panels with quatrefoil devices with rosettes; Gothic molding

OM-62 Reverse and repeat running ornament above a cornice: from center out: anthemion, volute, torche, volute, foliated ornament, plain patera

OM-63 Bottom right: Vitruvian scroll; upper left: egg-and-dart molding. Fascia above and below ornamented molding

OM-64 Stone molding. Top to bottom: egg-and-dart, dentil band, fascia, egg-and-dart ovolo, foliated band, leaf- or heart-and-dart, fascia between two bead-and-reel moldings

OM-65 Cornice on console. Top to bottom: anthemion cyma recta, leaf-and-dart cyma reversa, modillion band, egg-and-dart ovolo molding, dentil band

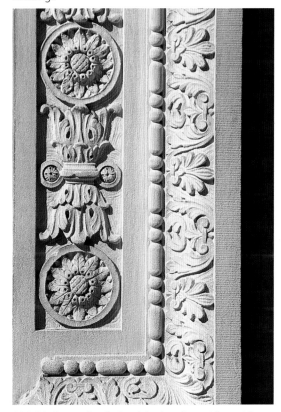

OM-66 Corner detail of enriched ovolo molding with trailing foliated pattern; bead-and-reel framing foliated design flanked by rosettes

MOLDING

OM-67 Entablature. Top to bottom: leaf-and-dart, plain corona, cyma, dentil band, egg-and-dart molding, foliated frieze, modified tongue-and-dart cymatium. Capital: egg-and-dart echinus, bead-and-reel, anthemion cavetto

OM-68 Simple Attic base with torus, fillet, scotia, torus, plinth

OM-69 Stepped fascia moldings, inset panels, corbelled block, and modillion-like elements

OM-70 Cornice. Top to bottom: plain ovolo molding, dentil band, plain cyma reversa, plain cyma recta

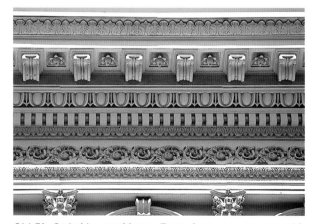

OM-71 Corinthian entablature. Top to bottom: cyma recta with anthemion, rosette-and-modillion cornice, egg-and-dart ovolo molding, dentil band, foliated frieze, tongue-and-dart cyma reversa

OM-72 Corner detail of egg-and-dart ovolo molding

OM-73 Metal cladding suggesting a frieze and cornice, "entablature" broken at corner to reveal the soffit of the "cornice," modern building facade

OM-74 Metal fascia bands suggesting molding, modern building facade

OM-75 Corner detail of metal fascia bands suggesting a classical entablature, the continuation of mullions suggesting a modillion band

OM-76 Metal panel with fascia framing bead molding, modern facade

OM-77 Cast metal molding. Top to bottom: cyma recta, cove, stepped fillets, cavetto, cyma recta, cyma reversa

OM-78 Metal fascia bands suggesting a classical entablature, broken at the division between bays (detail of OM-75)

MOLDING

OM-79 Metal molding in a panelized wall system resembling an exaggerated bead molding flattened when it turns the corner

OM-80 Stone base molding with a large bead and plinth with a chamfered top edge

OM-81 Abstracted cornice with a suggestion of a dentil band

OM-82 Dentilated cornice with enriched moldings; crossette over window (left)

OM-83 Top to bottom: modillion band; frieze with Greek-key pattern; foliated arabesque capital; banded neck; rusticated corner pier

OM-84 Doric entablature with block modillion band and frieze with discs in metopes alternating with triglyphs

OM-85 Top to bottom: heart-and-dart ogee, egg-and-dart ovolo moldings, plain frieze, leaf-and-dart moldings

MOLDING

OM-86 Triglyphs with guttae alternating with plain metopes; mutules with guttae in the soffit

OM-87 Ornamented corbelled courses. Top to bottom: Gothic cornice, three rows of billet molding, zigzag band, Gothic cornice

OM-88 Cornice. Top to bottom: serpentine band; modillion band; Gothic cornice. Dentilated archivolt at bottom

OM-89 Polychrome quatrefoil motif on a circular rose window, with acanthus motif on reverse ogee

OM-90 Top to bottom: Corinthian cornice; block modillions between coffers with rosettes; egg- and leaf-and-dart moldings, simple fascia, bead-and-reel molding, tongue-and-dart molding

OM-91 Cornice with simple modillions

OM-92 Classical entablature: plain architrave, no frieze, modillion band on cornice on weathered tin facade. Weathered tin Corinthian capitals

OM-93 Corner detail of Corinthian entablature: plain frieze and moldings; rosettes in coffers and in the soffit between the modillions

OM-94 Architrave with sculpted and inscribed frieze, modillion band; figurative sculpture in tympanum

OM-95 Weathered Ionic entablature with remains of a dentil band and an egg-and-dart ovolo molding below it

OM-96 Doric entablature: wreaths substituted for two triglyphs in the frieze; plain mutules in the soffit

OM-97 Vertical reeded band below modillion band and on neck of pilaster capital

OM-98 Weathered Corinthian cornice with inset panels in the frieze

OM-99 Two cornices, the lower supported by flat pilasters with molded imposts with scalloped dentil motif; balustrade in the frieze position

OM-100 Corinthian entablature with a vine-like guilloche in an otherwise plain frieze; modillions in traditional scroll profile

ENTABLATURE

OM-101 Frieze with a continuous figurative relief on the cornice

OM-102 Entablature with Doric features: triglyphs alternating with heraldic ornament in the frieze, quasi-dentil band, and soffit without mutules. Stylized Corinthian capital

OM-103 Corinthian entablature. Top to bottom: block modillions alternating with rosettes in corona soffit; plain frieze

OM-104 Two-banded architrave, festooned frieze flanking Corinthian pilasters

ENTABLATURE

Photo: Peter Miller

OM-105 Roman Doric–style entablature; discs in metopes; rosettes in coffers alternating with plain mutules in the soffit

OM-106 Three-banded architrave, plain shallow soffit; raised panels surrounded by leaf-and-dart molding over architrave

OM-107 Two-banded architrave with rosettes, leaf-and-dart molding, cavetto cornice with anthemions

Photo: Peter Miller

OM-108 Greek Doric–style entablature: plain architrave, triglyphs and plain metopes in the frieze, mutules with guttae in the soffit

ENTABLATURE

COLUMNS, POSTS & ARCHES

Photo: Austin, Patterson, Disston

Photo: Peter Miller

CP-1 Column c. 1920 in Greek Doric style with a smooth stucco finish

CP-2 Ionic capital and entablature with Greek styling

CP-3 Doric capital with Roman styling, egg-and-dart motif in echinus; rosettes on neck of engaged column

CP-4 Ionic capital with Roman styling

CP-5 Ionic capital with festoon between the eyes of the volutes and ornament on abacus

CP-6 Angular capital with rosette motif on necking and festoon on abacus

CAPITALS

CP-7 Adaptation of a Corinthian capital in Romanesque or Byzantine style

CP-8 Composite capital with idiosyncratic necking between astragal and acanthus leaves

CP-9 Corinthian capital and entablature

CP-10 Corinthian capital and entablature

Photo: Peter Miller

Photo: Peter Miller

CAPITALS

CP-11 Doric capital with Roman proportions; characteristic Greek groove replacing astragal molding

CP-12 Tuscan capital under an overhang with balustrade

CP-13 Romanesque- or Byzantine-style adaptation of a Corinthian capital

CAPITALS

CP-14 Modern derivatives of Byzantine-style square capitals serving as imposts on octagonal shafts

CP-15 Modern derivative of early French Gothic–style capital with acanthus motif and oversized impost

CP-16 Capital with lotus and acanthus leaves, derivative of ancient Greek style

CP-17 Tuscan capital on corner pilaster

CAPITALS

CP-18 Roman-style Doric capitals on adjacent engaged column and pilaster, egg-and-dart echinus, and typical Doric entablature

CP-19 Corinthian capital on flat pilaster below weathered entablature with egg-and-dart and dentilated moldings

CP-20 Romanesque capitals on a series of pilasters and jamb-shafts in compound arch

CAPITALS

CP-21 Capital with profile derivative of Doric capital; necking ornamented with anthemion on a square corner pier with dentilated molding

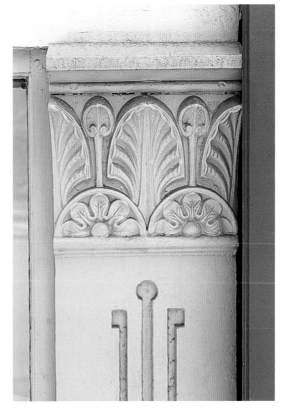

CP-22 Cast-iron pilaster and capital with lotus motif

CP-23 Byzantine- or Egyptian-style capital on smooth jamb-shaft in portal

CP-24 American-order capital and entablature with egg-and-dart molding, arabesque frieze, and block modillions

CAPITALS

CP-25 Ionic capital with fluted necking on pilaster

CP-26 Idiosyncratic angle capitals with fluted necking on corner pilaster

Photo: Guy Gurney

CP-27 Ancient capital

CAPITALS

CP-28 Modern square capital with fluting

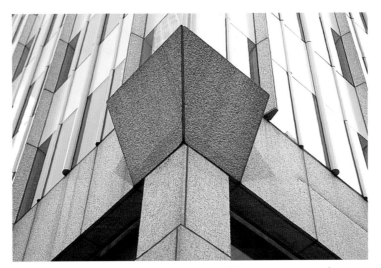

CP-29 Abstract geometric reference to a capital in stone veneer, modern commercial building

CP-30 Art Deco–style capital in glass and metal with non-regular octagonal profile, lit from inside

CAPITALS

CP-31 Idiosyncratic marble Attic base with foliated ornament draped over torus on plinth

CP-32 Attic base of weathered column in volcanic stone with banded rusticated shaft

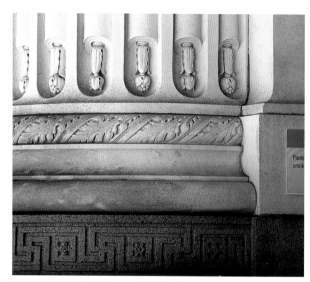

CP-33 Marble Attic base with foliated ornament on upper torus on plinth in contrasting stone with Greek-key molding; ornamented fluting

CP-34 Attic base on a thin plinth. Top to bottom: torus; fillet; scotia; fillet; torus

Photo: Guy Gurney

CP-35 Doric base of heavily weathered volcanic stone column on square plinth

CP-36 Attic base of weathered travertine column on square plinth

CP-37 Attic base of travertine engaged column on octagonal plinth

CP-38 Attic base on square plinth with detail of fluting

CP-39 Weathered marble column with Attic base on stepped octagonal plinth; right: brick pilaster on square marble base

CP-40 Left: marble pier base with Attic profile and ogee molding below plinth; right: jamb-shafts with Attic-profile bases above plinths

BASES & PEDESTALS

CP-41 Medieval column and base on volcanic stone plinth

CP-42 Banded brick and stone jamb-shafts; base with shallow, elongated scotia over torus on plinth with scalloped corner

CP-43 Square pilaster with typical Roman Corinthian Ionic base; mason's miter on outside corner

CP-44 Travertine column on Attic base on square stepped plinth

BASES & PEDESTALS

CP-45 Banded granite veneer pilaster on Tuscan-style base, entry of modern commercial building

CP-46 Square pier on base of granite veneer with geometric abstraction of a scalloped plinth, portico of modern commercial building

CP-47 Pier of granite veneer on Tuscan-style base, entry of modern commercial building

CP-48 Banded stone-veneer pier on base, grouted corner and joints, modern commercial building

BASES & PEDESTALS

CP-49 Hand-hewn beveled timber post on a honed stone base with rounded edge

CP-50 Marble column with compound square base. Left: Attic profile base on a high plinth; right: Attic profile

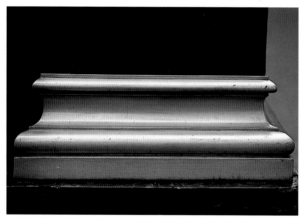

CP-51 Square metal base, Attic profile with enlarged scotia and diminished upper torus

CP-52 Timber post on a square chamfered stone base

CP-53 Natural boulders supporting timber posts under deck of pavilion in Japanese garden pond

CP-54 Gilded relief ornamental metal sheath covering the base of a timber post

CP-55 Heavily weathered painted octagonal wood base in Carpenter Gothic style

CP-56 Timber post on square stone base with carved design, Indonesia

CP-57 Timber post on stone base with carved animal design, Indonesia

BASES & PEDESTALS

CP-58 Heavily weathered marble ancient Roman fluted column with Attic base

CP-59 Fluted column with Doric base on round pedestal with Attic base and floral ornament

CP-60 Marble Salomonic column shaft with Cosmatesque fluting

CP-61 Bundled terracotta shafts. Left: chevron pattern; right: reticulated pattern

CP-62 Heavily weathered ancient Roman column with remnants of Attic base

CP-63 Cast-iron column with Doric/Tuscan base and a band of round ornaments on round pedestal with Attic base

CP-64 Wreathed column in mosaic with floral design

COLUMNS

CP-65 Center: partially fluted shafts with band of anthemion ornament and visible joints between drums; right: flat pilaster with brick and ornamented bands

CP-66 Partially fluted and banded Corinthian columns with relief ornament

CP-67 Stone entryway with partially fluted Salomonic columns, garland ornament, and Composite capitals

CP-68 Gothic-style jamb-shafts with annulets, varied shaft treatments: spiral fluting and stepped helical geometric pattern

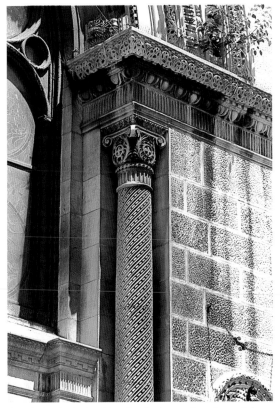

CP-69 Jamb-shaft with spiral fluting and angle capital with volutes

CP-70 Corinthian columns with fluted shafts

CP-71 Corner cluster of three columns with unresolved capitals

CP-72 Corinthian columns with partially fluted shafts next to flat pilasters

COLUMNS

CP-73 Roman-style Doric columns with Attic base supporting portico; pedimented door

CP-74 Corinthian columns supporting portico

CP-75 Marble Ionic columns with fluted shafts; wall with bull's-eye windows; marble entablature

COLUMNS

CP-76 Double row of Ionic columns with plain entablature

CP-77 Corinthian fluted columns with engraved entablature

CP-78 Ionic fluted column with pronounced entasis

CP-79 Greek Doric columns with typical entablature

CP-80 Pilasters with a mosaic zigzag pattern, restaurant facade

CP-81 Compound corner pier, modern commercial building

CP-82 Flush fluted pilasters with Corinthian-style capitals

CP-83 Antae of adjacent cast-iron buildings. Left: Corinthian pilaster with fluting; right: fluted shaft with eclectic capital and adjacent jamb-shaft

PILASTERS & ENGAGED COLUMNS

CP-84 Stone pilasters with flutes and banded rusticated bases

CP-85 Banded stone pilasters with raised vermiculated panels alternating with honed bands

CP-86 Glazed architectural terracotta Ionic pilasters with fluted shafts and angle-capitals; entablature with festoon, capped with balustrade

CP-87 Pilaster with trapezoidal profile, cabled, with a diminished capital resembling an Egyptian bell capital

CP-88 Weathered painted pilasters in a blind arcade with semicircular arches

CP-89 Stone pilasters with Byzantine or Romanesque capitals against windowed wall

CP-90 Brick pilaster with dentil motif at the capital and blind cambered or very shallow segmental arch; dentilated molding above arch

CP-91 Corinthian flat pilaster next to window in a Venetian arch

CP-92 Corinthian engaged columns

CP-93 Triplet of engaged Romanesque columns with foliated entablature

CP-94 Rusticated engaged banded Doric column and pilaster; Doric-style entablature

CP-95 Ionic engaged columns with polished granite shafts

PILASTERS & ENGAGED COLUMNS

CP-96 Reticulated colonnettes (jamb-shafts) in a portal with annulets

CP-97 Fluted and reeded pilasters on Art Deco facade

CP-98 Bundled pier on modern commercial building

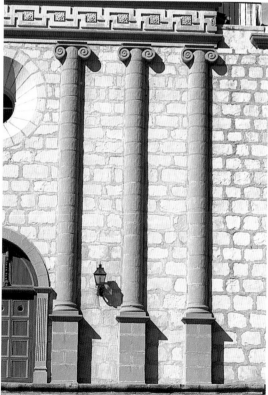

CP-99 Engaged Ionic columns and decorated entablature, 19th-c. American Southwestern mission

PILASTERS & ENGAGED COLUMNS

CP-100 Bundled banded piers in a Romanesque-style facade, modern commercial building

CP-101 Ancient Roman marble Ionic engaged column

CP-102 Brick engaged columns flanking gauged-brick semi-circular arch windows

CP-103 Banded and rock-pitched engaged Corinthian capitals below entablature with stylized keystones

CP-104 Ionic engaged columns with entablature and festooned spandrels

PILASTERS & ENGAGED COLUMNS

CP-105 Timber post with mortise-and-through-tenon joint

CP-106 Timber post connected to stone plinth with rabbeted scarf joint and metal hoops. Horizontal brace joined by mortise-and-through-tenon joint

CP-107 Intersection of post and beam. Post appears to go directly through a mortise and is held in place by decorative tie irons

CP-108 Timber post with a horizontal brace attached by a double-wedged through-tenon joint with metal stripping on the top

POSTS & BEAMS

CP-109 Timber lintel in stone wall

CP-110 Timber corner post with two offset mortise-and-tenon connections
to beams

CP-111 Keyed mortise-and-tenon joint between a post and a rail

CP-112 Steel frame and tubular column; wide-flange beams supporting framed glass ceiling of modern commercial building

CP-113 Painted metal beam with welded connections; painted corrugated metal walls

CP-114 Painted poured-in-place concrete pier supporting a steel frame with cladding finished with spray-on stucco

CP-115 Poured-in-place concrete piers supporting deep steel plate girders

CP-116 Hammer-beam sitting on post supporting a beam above

CP-117 Piers built up from split-faced stone or concrete, modern commercial building

CP-118 Painted metal beam with welded and riveted connections; painted corrugated metal walls

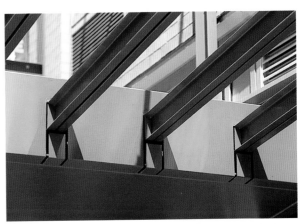

CP-119 Steel beams built up of two C-channels of weathering steel

CP-120 Post-and-beam construction with polychrome ornamental brackets, Japanese temple

CP-121 Semicircular metal canopy supported by a metal bracket set into a masonry column, modern commercial building

Photo: Austin, Patterson, Disston

CP-122 Painted steel frame with wide-flange beams and riveted connections, supporting corrugated steel decking, ceiling of modern house

CP-123 Detail of steel frame with metal-clad column and beam beneath exposed riveted plate girders, modern commercial building

CP-124 Steel frame clad with possibly stainless steel panels, modern commercial building

CP-125 Painted steel truss of riveted plates, industrial building

CP-126 Steel or concrete piers with polished stone and metal cladding, modern commercial building

CP-127 Polygonal concrete pier supporting overhang, reflecting pool in modern commercial building

CP-128 Rectangular stone-veneer pier with articulated corners supporting portico, modern commercial building

CP-129 Steel column with stainless-steel cladding supporting entry canopy, modern commercial building

CP-130 Exposed corner octagonal pier with stone veneer

CP-131 Pier with metal post and stone cladding supporting entry canopy, modern commercial building

CP-132 Concrete column and beams, possibly pre-cast, supporting waffle slab

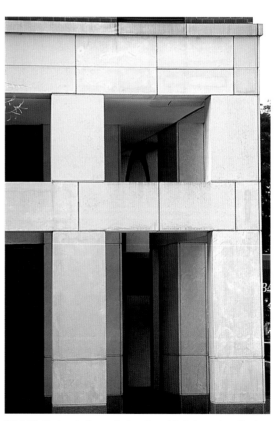

CP-133 Trabeated arcade (post-and-lintel construction), modern commercial building

CP-134 Timber post on turned stone base supporting roof of veranda

CP-135 Banded vermiculated coquina pilasters on square posts, garden arcade

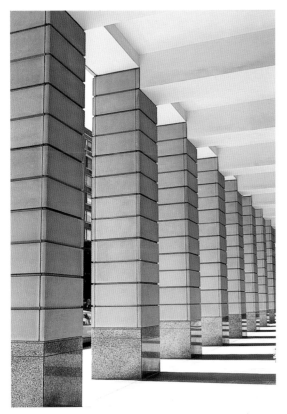

CP-136 Polished rusticated granite-veneer piers with adjoining boxed beams in arcade, modern commercial building

CP-137 Stone post with Attic base supporting wooden garden trellis

CP-138 Steel frame with metal-clad column and beam beneath exposed riveted plate girders, modern commercial building

CP-139 Brick piers with dog-tooth courses

CP-140 Post-and-beam construction, Japanese temple

POSTS & BEAMS

CP-141 Semicircular arch with an ancon keystone on masonry running-bond wall with Vitruvian scroll trim and rosette medallions

CP-142 Semicircular arches with voussoirs and archivolt, carved spandrel, and dentilated molding

CP-143 Semicircular arch in stucco wall with molded impost blocks, archivolt, and inset wrought-iron tracery

CP-144 Arcade of semicircular compound arches; spandrels with cartouches and foliated ornament

CP-145 Archivolt continuous with architrave; pediment over the door

ARCHES

CP-146 Semicircular arch around window with ornamented keystone, rope and foliated moldings

CP-147 Bell arch with corbels, geometric archivolt surrounded by patterned terracotta

CP-148 Arcade of semicircular arches, rope molding in intrados, square panel rosettes, and quatrefoil medallion in spandrel

CP-149 Compound arch with carved archivolts

ARCHES

CP-150 Rustic semicircular masonry arch in rubble wall in natural rock formation

CP-151 Moorish horseshoe arch with terracotta archivolt

CP-152 Stepped freestanding arch with cartouche over keystone

CP-153 Semicircular Roman brick arch in random rubble wall

CP-154 Florentine arch (extrados and intrados not concentric), gauged brick. Extrados emphasized with a molding

CP-155 Two-centered surbased arch (arch rising less than half its span) in castle entry under corbelled jetty

ARCHES

CP-156 Terracotta wall and semicircular arch with ornamented tympanum

CP-157 Semicircular gauged-brick arch over entryway

CP-158 Shallow surbased arch in rubble masonry with wood door

CP-159 Semicircular compound arch with carved relief sculpture in tympanum

CP-160 Weathered stucco-covered stone semicircular arch with wood double doors, rustic courtyard

CP-161 Windows in semicircular arch; extrados with carved molding terminating at capitals

ARCHES

CP-162 Carpenter Gothic arcade with trefoil arches, quatrefoil ornaments in spandrels

CP-163 Arcade with Islamic-style surbased arches (the three on left, ogee arches); Byzantine capitals on square columns

CP-164 Arcade with semicircular arches with molding at springing, stucco over adobe brick, late-18th-c. American Southwestern mission

CP-165 Semicircular arcade, stucco over brick; tile roof

Photo: Guy Gurney

CP-166 Groin-vaulted arcade with multipart vaults and arches

ARCHES

CP-167 Three levels of weathered ancient Roman arches

CP-168 Rusticated coquina garden portal with semicircular stepped arch, crossettes, banding, and ornamented balustrade with a mascaron

Photo: Guy Gurney

CP-169 Gothic arcade with ribbed vaulting

ARCHES

CP-170 Semicircular arch enclosing three compound pointed trefoil arched windows below sexfoil and two trefoil ornaments, with balustrade

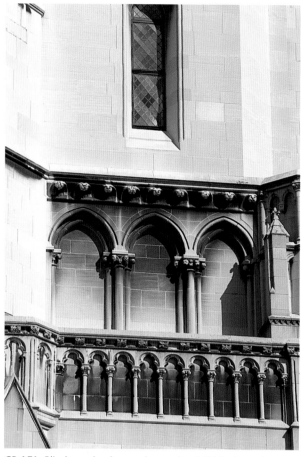

CP-171 Blind arcade: drop arches and trefoil blind arcade on Gothic-style facade

CP-172 Blind arcade: basket-handle (three-centered arch) stone arches with ornament, late-18th-c. courtyard

ARCHES

CP-173 Upper-story blind arcade of semicircular arches with coats-of-arms

CP-174 Fenestrated arcade of semicircular arches framing embrasure windows

CP-175 Arcade of Tudor arches with tracery

ARCHES

185

CP-176 Barrel-vaulted metal and glass modern greenhouse structure

CP-177 Barrel-vaulted tubular-steel-frame-and-glass entry, modern commercial building

CP-178 Multiple levels of arcades, modern apartment house

ARCHES

WINDOWS

WI-1 Leaded roundels

WI-2 Leaded window with decorative cames in stone arch

WI-3 Leaded casement window with cames in diamond lattice pattern

WI-4 Leaded glass with octagonal brass muntins in interlocking pattern

WI-5 Fixed window with brass muntins and mullion, modern commercial building

WI-6 Fixed window with stainless steel muntins and mullions, modern commercial building

WI-7 Stainless steel muntins, modern commercial building

WI-8 Metal muntins holding weathered translucent glass, industrial building

MULLIONS, MUNTINS & LEADED GLASS

WI-9 Leaded colored and textured glass, 20th-c. American house

WI-10 Figured glass with a pattern of different textures

WI-11 Figured glass with flat metal muntins in a metal frame, industrial building

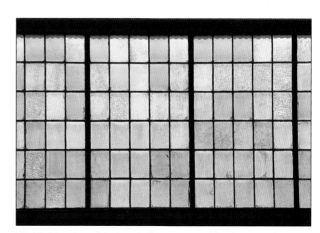

WI-12 Muntins with tinted glass separated by three mullions, industrial building

WI-13 Tinted and weathered glass, factory windows

WI-14 Etched design in clear glass on frosted ground

WI-15 Colored glass in stainless steel frame in lower window and gable wall, modern mixed-use building

WI-16 Colored and clear fixed and casement windows (note floor plate behind the middle windows), modern house

WI-17 Bronze mirror-glass windows in curtain wall, modern commercial building

WI-18 Antique colored glass, lobby of 19th-c. mixed-use building

COLORED & TEXTURED GLASS

WI-19 Detail of glass-block corner window

WI-20 Stepped window in clear and frosted glass block with ceramic tile central panel, modern house

WI-21 Glass-block panels spanning two stories and flanked by fixed windows, modern commercial building

WI-22 Undulating window: flat and curved glass block with wavy texture, Art Deco apartment building

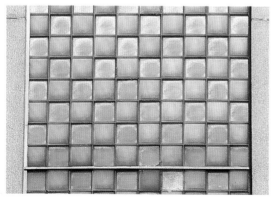

WI-23 Linear textured blocks in checkerboard pattern, 20th-c. mixed-use building

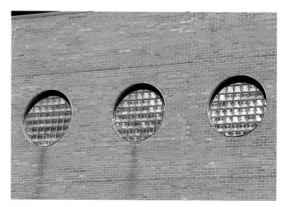

WI-24 Circular windows with glass block, modern commercial building

GLASS BLOCK

WI-25 Two double-casement windows with divided transom lights, stone window surrounds, 19th-c. apartment house

WI-26 Wood-framed awning windows with carved transom panel, Balinese house

WI-27 Leaded double-casement windows with cames in a diamond pattern, 16th-c. half-timbered English house

WI-28 Wood-framed awning windows with shaped wood muntins, Arts and Crafts house

WI-29 Venetian-style casement windows with pilasters between windows

TYPES OF WINDOWS

WI-30 Six- and ten-light double-casement windows with fly-screen insets in three windows, 19th-c. town house

WI-31 Casement windows with internal muntins and fixed light above, modern metal replacement windows in older apartment house

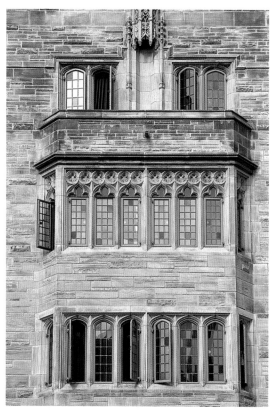

WI-32 Leaded casement windows in neo-Gothic bay window; middle windows with stone tracery

WI-33 Two- and three-light double-casement windows

TYPES OF WINDOWS

WI-34 Leaded casement windows, top set in wall dormer, stone house

WI-35 Split-casement windows with wood frames in stone wall

WI-36 Double-casement window in stucco wall

WI-37 Awning windows in curved corner, Art Deco apartment house

TYPES OF WINDOWS

WI-38 Casement or awning windows set in fixed windows with probably extruded aluminum framing, modern townhouse

WI-39 Casement windows (center) and awning window (left) set in fixed lights; extruded aluminum mullions, modern apartment house

WI-40 Fully glazed wood sliding door, surrounded by fixed lights or awning windows, modern house

WI-41 Stacked awning windows

WI-42 Single-hung or awning windows with various muntin patterns, modern apartment house

WI-43 Awning windows, modern metal-clad house

TYPES OF WINDOWS

WI-44 One-over-one double-hung windows

WI-45 Twelve-over-twelve double-hung window, American stone house

WI-46 Six-over-six double-hung window with stone lintel in weathered brick wall

WI-47 Four-over-four double-hung windows with crown molding, 19th-c. American clapboard house

TYPES OF WINDOWS

WI-48 Double-hung windows: seven-over-seven decorative lights; one-over-one with shutters

WI-49 Top to bottom: arched gable window; arched six-over-one double-hung windows; six-over-one double-hung windows, traditional shingle house

WI-50 Double-hung windows, 19th-c. clapboard church

TYPES OF WINDOWS

WI-51 Double-hung windows: one-over-one (left); sixteen-over-one (gable); one-over-one decorative-lights (right), 19th-c. clapboard house

WI-52 Double-hung windows: twenty-over-twenty with pilaster mullions (top); twenty-over-ones flanking twelve-over-twelve, 20th-c. shingle house

WI-53 Four-over-four double-hung windows with wood frames and modern storm windows, 19th-c. clapboard house

WI-54 Top: fixed Palladian window; bottom: six-over-six double-hung windows, American stone house

Photo: The Preservation Society of Newport County

TYPES OF WINDOWS

Photo: The Preservation Society of Newport County

WI-55 Curved double-hung windows with slumped glass. Top: fifteen-over-fifteen; bottom: twenty-five-over-one, 20th-c. American shingle house

WI-56 Double-hung metal or vinyl replacement windows with internal muntins, 19th-c. brick industrial building

WI-57 One-over-one double-hung metal or vinyl replacement windows, 19th-c. brick apartment building

WI-58 One-over-one double-hung, arched top sashes with fixed lights; fixed bull's eye window above

TYPES OF WINDOWS

WI-59 Fixed hexagonal windows, modern commercial building

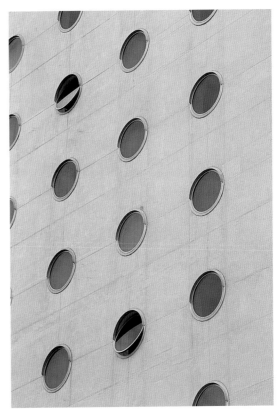

WI-60 Circular awning windows with stainless steel frames, modern commercial building

WI-61 Oval bull's-eye windows with foliated marble frames and festoons, 19th-c. mansion

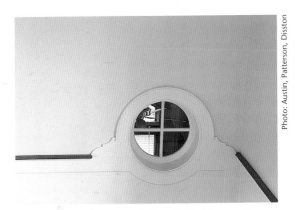

WI-62 Circular clerestory window divided by muntins, with a flat wood profiled frame, modern house

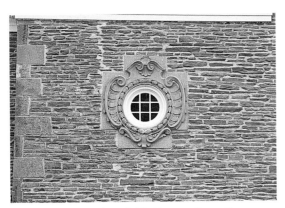

WI-63 Circular window divided by muntins, with a carved stone frame

WI-64 Bull's-eye dormer- and wall windows, with one square window

WI-65 Circular window divided by radiating muntins with ventilation opening above in stone gable wall

WI-66 Oval window divided by muntins, with flat wood casing in white cedar-shingle gable wall

WI-67 Rose window with stone tracery

WI-68 Oval window divided by flat muntins; foliated stone frame with ancon flanked by festoons

TYPES OF WINDOWS

WI-69 Fixed windows with lattice in top lights, modern house

WI-70 Fixed window with internal muntins, fanlight, and shutters in stucco gable wall

WI-71 Oval, rectangular, and arched fixed windows, Mediterranean-style modern house

WI-72 Arched and geometric fixed windows, modern house

TYPES OF WINDOWS

WI-73 Geometric fixed windows, modern house

WI-74 Fixed tinted windows in stainless steel frames on curved wall, modern commercial building

WI-75 Fixed windows and sidelights; awnings with brackets, patio wall of modern house

TYPES OF WINDOWS

WI-76 Stone oriel, 18th-c. English house

WI-77 Cant-bay window: six-over-six, double-hung, with wood casings, brick base, and flared standing-seam roof, traditional house

WI-78 Wood corner oriel: one-over-one, double-hung, wood sashes and casings, conical flat-seamed copper roof, 19th-c. American mixed-use building

WI-79 Brick corner two-story oriel: one-over-one double-hung windows below and arched window with decorative lights (left), 19th-c. commercial building

BAY & CORNER WINDOWS

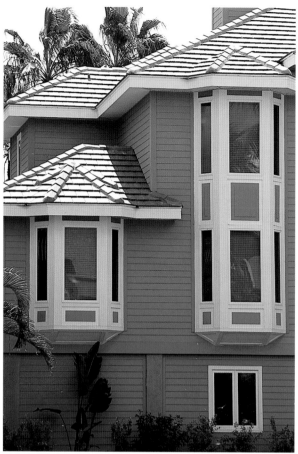

WI-80 Single- and two-story oriels with fixed windows, modern house

WI-81 Metal-clad two-story angled bay. Top: fixed windows with awning lights; bottom: one-over-one double-hung sashes, modern apartment house

WI-82 Cant-sided bay with three windows per side, conical shingle roof, modern house

Photo: Roger Bartels Architects, Dobyan & Dobyan Custom Builders

BAY & CORNER WINDOWS

WI-83 Two-story cant-bay windows: fixed lights below ornamental cast or pressed metalwork, apartment house

WI-84 Left: double-casement window; right: cant-oriel with fixed side and transom lights and center casement window, 19th-c. mixed-use building

WI-85 Stone cant-oriel: leaded casement windows under tracery lights; roof balustrade; bas-relief ornamental band below window

BAY & CORNER WINDOWS

WI-86 Corner window: fixed lights with metal sashes, muntins, and mullions, modern commercial building

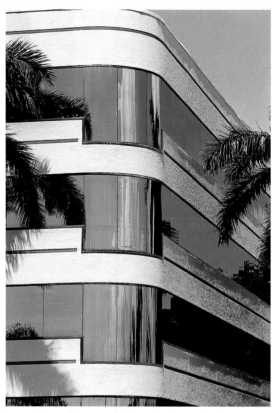

WI-87 Curved corner windows with strip windows; tinted plate glass, modern commercial building

WI-88 Curved corner strip windows, modern commercial building

WI-89 Corner windows: double casement with side lights and split transom lights, Art Deco apartment house

BAY & CORNER WINDOWS

WI-90 Idiosyncratic bay with fixed lights, modern commercial building

WI-91 Corner windows: single-hung sashes with fixed upper lights, Art Deco apartment house

WI-92 Oriel with awning or fixed windows, shed roof, and corbels, modern apartment house

WI-93 Idiosyncratic fixed-light bay with mirror-glass top section, modern commercial building

BAY & CORNER WINDOWS

Photo: Austin, Patterson, Disston

WI-94 Segmental-arch transom light with shingle "voussoirs" and "keystone" above French door, modern shingle house

WI-95 Shaped stone transom light over French door with side lights under engaged balcony

WI-96 Fanlight in Palladian window with fixed leaded lights and stone frame

WI-97 Fanlight over fifteen-over-fifteen double-hung wood window

TRANSOM LIGHTS & FANLIGHTS

WI-98 Fanlight with ornamental metal grille

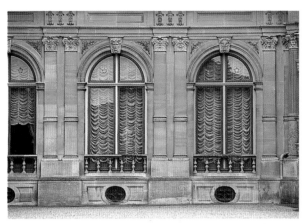

WI-99 Semicircular-arch transom lights over French doors in stone surround with keystones and pilasters, English house

WI-100 Semicircular-arch fanlights over square fixed lights, with one-over-one double-hung sashes and window gates, 19th-c. townhouse

WI-101 Leaded rectangular transom lights over casement windows; hood supported by brackets, Arts and Crafts house

WI-102 Top to bottom: rectangular transom lights; fixed lights; pairs of one-over-one double-hung windows and fixed side lights, modern apartment house

WI-103 Bat-wing fanlight under pediment

WI-104 Segmental pediment-capped window molding with consoles flanking double-hung windows, 19th-c. American house

Photo: Austin, Patterson, Disston

WI-105 Flat wood casing around double-hung windows in stucco and brick wall, traditional house

WI-106 Flat wood casing around double-casement windows

WI-107 Flat wood casing with crossettes around one-over-one double-hung windows; hood supported by brackets, American clapboard house

WI-108 Flat trim echoing arch profiles of window openings, American brick house

WI-109 Flat trim echoing arch profiles of window openings, 19th-c. American mixed-use building

WI-110 Wood gable-shaped hood over double-hung window, American clapboard house

WI-111 Variety of fenestrations: six-over-six double-hung windows in half-timber–style gable wall, traditional house

WI-112 Ornament and molding around group of three double-hung windows; consoles supporting cornice, 19th-c. American stone commercial building

WI-113 Profiled flat casing around double-casement window

WI-114 Flat casing around corner windows and horizontal window, modern shingle house

Photo: Austin, Patterson, Disston

Photo: Roger Bartels Architects, Dobyan & Dobyan Builders

WI-115 Round pediment over gable double-hung dormer window flanked by pairs of attached columns

WI-116 Ornament, molding, and balustrade around double-hung windows in cant-bay and wall windows; 19th-c. American clapboard house

WI-117 Set of three gable wall double-hung windows; flat wood casings, with crown molding caps

WI-118 Gauged-brick jack arch, brick quoins, and "keystone" in contrasting color

WI-119 Gauged-brick segmental-arch windows with brick quoins and "keystones" in contrasting color

WI-120 Masonry and tile band following profile of segmental arch

WI-121 Shaped embrasure in coursed-rubble wall, 19th-c. American Southwestern mission

WI-122 Segmental-arch-shaped casement window framed by brick arch and pilasters

WI-123 Stone flat keystone arches and quoins framing double-hung windows in coursed-rubble wall

WI-124 Stone lintels and carved casing tops with stone and brickwork band around double-hung windows in brick wall

WI-125 Stone classical-style window casings with crown molding capping lower window; consoles supporting sill and cornice

Photo: The Preservation Society of Newport County

WI-126 Stone cartouches flanking upper-story windows with molded casings, replacement windows, early 20th-c. apartment house

WI-127 Stone ornament around picture window and side windows separated by pilasters; top stone casing pierced with ogee arches

WI-128 Terracotta cornice with garlands around windows with terracotta casings; blind window under cartouche

WI-129 Windows with jack arches in roughly squared random stone wall

WI-130 Stone or cast concrete casings with relief ornament and ornamented keystones, early 20th-c. apartment house

WI-131 Set of three recessed windows with stone molded casings and single molded sill, early 20th-c. commercial building

WINDOW TRIM & FENESTRATION

WI-132 Stone classical casing around shuttered window, old Roman building

WI-133 Marble pediment and pilasters framing carved marble casing with polychrome marble bands, 12th-c. Italian church

WI-134 Stone eclectic ornament flanking metal replacement window, apartment house

WI-135 Stone pointed segmental arch framing pair of leaded lancet windows with stone casings and leaded quatrefoil, 15th-c. English abbey

WI-136 Polychrome ornamented architectural terracotta frame around stone casings, apartment building

WI-137 Fanciful neo-Gothic spandrel with cartouche flanked by corbelled pilasters, apartment building

WI-138 Set of three dormer windows with stone casing flanked by pilasters in half-timber–style gable with engaged balustrade

WI-139 Scrolled pediment with cartouche, engaged columns, and balustrade below window with side lights, apartment house

WI-140 Ornamented brownstone voussoirs around semi-circular-arch window

WI-141 Neo-Gothic ornament in spandrels and capping window panels, early 20th-c. commercial building

WI-142 Ornamental semicircular arches capping pair of arched windows separated by single engaged column; bottom cartouche panels

WI-143 Series of arches, pilasters, and polychrome terra-cotta or stone spandrels framing windows in stone casing, 19th-c. French mixed-use building

WI-144 Framed bas-relief tympanums and ornamented pilasters around windows; blind-arch window with glazed tile

WI-145 Assortment of moldings and ornament around square casement windows over profiled fixed window

WI-146 Metal spandrel with relief design and metal casings

WI-147 Metal spandrels with cast relief designs and metal casings

WI-148 Stone arch around fixed lancet-shaped and circular lights

WI-149 Copper panels capping windows with metal sashes in recessed stone casings, 20th-c. commercial building

WI-150 Relief ornamental panel and pilasters around variation of Venetian-style window with balcony; 20th-c. apartment house

WI-151 Horizontal stacked wood board surround around fixed-light window, modern commercial building

WI-152 Square casement window recessed in stucco wall above arch; painted Spanish-colonial–style motifs

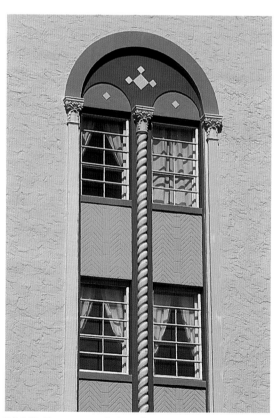

WI-153 Two-story variation of Venetian-style window; painted stucco and cast-concrete ornament, Art Deco hotel

WI-154 Variety of fenestrations of rectangular, probably fixed, windows, modern commercial building

WI-155 Repetitive fenestration of metal-framed windows in banded facade design, modern commercial building

WI-156 Repetitive fenestration of picture windows with side lights and double-hung windows (right) with brick quoins, modern commercial building

WI-157 Metal design in spandrels connecting upper and lower windows

WI-158 Repetitive fenestration of three-mullion windows with raised panel spandrels, modern commercial building

WI-159 Banded fenestration: row of arched windows and rows of square windows; metal replacement windows, 19th-c. industrial building

WI-160 Stone spandrels dividing recessed square metal fixed windows, modern commercial building

WI-161 Group of fixed windows with two louvered ventilation panels in stone surround, modern commercial building

WI-162 Interlocking design of square windows with metal spandrels and surround, modern commercial building

WI-163 Repetitive fenestration with open and closed window shades, modern apartment building

WI-164 Mirror-glass strip windows, modern commercial building

WI-165 Mirror-glass strip windows, modern commercial building

WI-166 Ribbon windows separated by solid panels, modern apartment building

WI-167 Stainless steel window gate

WI-168 Painted wrought-iron window grille with decorative border

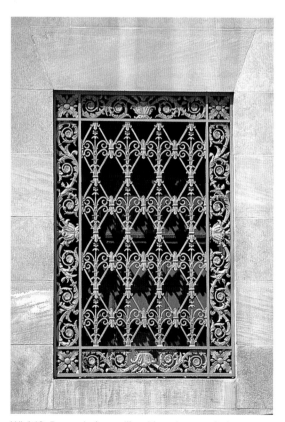

WI-169 Brass window grille with arabesque design around pierced diaper-work

WI-170 Wrought-iron window gates with diaper pattern, modern apartment house

WI-171 Patinated filigree metal grille

WI-172 Brass grille with interlocking hexagon-and-star pattern

WI-173 Pierced marble grille with diaper pattern

WI-174 Bamboo grille in diagonal design

WI-175 Wrought-iron window gate in Spanish-colonial style

WI-176 Grille of turned wood bars, American Southwestern mission

WI-177 Rustic wood grille

WI-178 Traditional Japanese lattice window grille

WI-179 Metal shutters, 19th-c. industrial building

WI-180 Weathered double-hinged louvered shutters

WI-181 Weathered metal awning

WI-182 Pairs of framed louvered shutters

WI-183 Louvered shutters with fixed top shutters

WI-184 Louvered shutters with fixed top shutters

WI-185 Double-hinged louvered shutters

WI-186 Louvered shutters

WI-187 Rustic louvered shutters

WI-188 Modern plastic louvered shutters

SHUTTERS

WI-189 Rustic battened shutters

WI-190 Battened shutters

WI-191 Horizontal-board shutters with pierced design

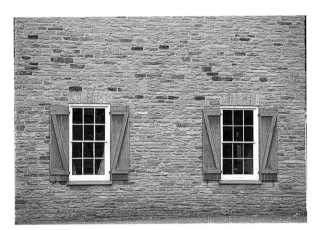

WI-192 Shutters with Z-battens

WI-193 Battened shutters and door

WI-194 Weathered painted metal shutter

WI-195 Raised-panel shutter with cutout

WI-196 Rustic warehouse shutters

WI-197 Weathered painted wood paneled shutters

WI-198 Louvered and paneled shutters

WI-199 Planked shutter, Japanese house

WI-200 Louvered shutters with upper lights

WI-201 Sliding lattice shutter, Japanese house

WI-202 Sun screens of translucent panels, modern mixed-use building

WI-203 Hurricane shutters, modern apartment house

WI-204 Skylight shutters, modern commercial building

SHUTTERS

DOORWAYS

DW-1 Three narrow panels, wood, with leaded lights, brass handle, decorative plates and studs on stiles, panels, and rails; segmental-arch doorway

DW-2 Twenty-one panels, wood, with leaded light, mail slot, and decorative studs on rails and stiles

DW-3 Six panels, wood; double doors with carved diamond pattern in panels, ornament framing handles, studded bottom panel, and transom grille

DW-4 Fifteen wood and open-grilled panels, studs on painted stiles and rails; segmental-arch doorway

PANELED DOORS

DW-5 Four panels, wood double doors with flush molding and raised panels

DW-6 Wood with geometric patterned panels. Left: etched glass; right: inlaid wood

DW-7 Six panels, unfinished wood double doors with planked panels and wrought-iron handles; metal door-frame with transom light and side lights

DW-8 Two panels, double doors with carved bas-relief ornament and trompe l'oeil wood finish. Cambered stone arch doorway with cartouche keystone

PANELED DOORS

DW-9 Two panels with applied trim; pilaster doorframe with anthemion on lintel; transom light and side lights

DW-10 Four diagonally planked panels, painted door with wrought-iron handle, clapboard house

DW-11 Single-panel double garage doors and single-panel door; unfinished wood veneer

PANELED DOORS

DW-12 Single-panel, book-matched wood with wrought-iron hardware, Japanese courtyard gate

DW-13 Weathered two-panel wood with double cross-braces, brass hardware, and doorknob in center stile, Japanese courtyard gate

DW-14 Single-panel double doors with polychrome bas-relief panels, Indonesian courtyard gate

DW-15 Five panels, wood double doors with diamond grille, Japanese temple

PANELED DOORS

Photo: Austin, Patterson, Disston

DW-16 Six-panel mahogany door with raised panels; side lights, residential front entry

DW-17 Six-panel wood door with raised panels, carved molding, and half-round transom light

DW-18 Wood garage doors with raised panels

PANELED DOORS

DW-19 Two-panel wood double doors with flush molding; upper panels glass, lower panels divided; letter slot in center stile; split transom light

DW-20 Painted wood door; ribbed-glass panel with nine lights; wood panels flush-molded; pilaster frame

DW-21 Wood double doors with glass upper panels and flush-molded lower panels; split transom light in segmen-

DW-22 Weathered wood double doors; single glass panels frosted and etched with zigzag and diaper patterns

PANELED DOORS

DW-23 Arch-shaped wood double doors with center pilaster; stucco surround, American Southwestern mission style

DW-24 Plain-sawn plank door with wrought-iron strap hinges; woven wood walls, 18th-c. corn crib

DW-25 Plain-sawn planks with double Z-brace, farm shed

DW-26 Weathered plank doors under rough-hewn timber lintel; rustic stone and stucco gable wall of barn and hayloft

BATTENED DOORS

DW-27 Oak door with leaded lights and ornate wrought-iron strap-hinges; arched transom panel

DW-28 Oak door with leaded-glass light, ornate brass strap hinges; segmental arch

DW-29 Stained wood courtyard gate with horizontal braces, set in painted stucco wall

BATTENED DOORS

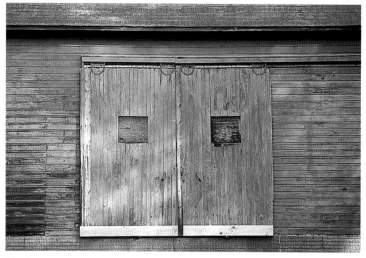

DW-30 Painted wood siding and hanging double doors on weathered barn

DW-31 Wood double garage doors with lights and curved Z-braces in field-stone wall, Arts and Crafts house

DW-32 Wood double garage doors with diagonal planking, in segmental arch

BATTENED DOORS

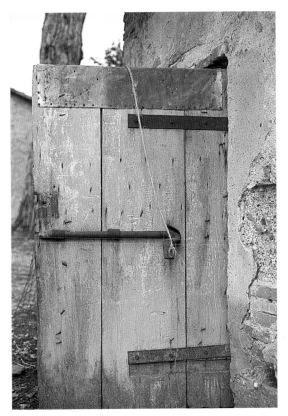

DW-33 Weathered painted wood-plank door with rustic iron strap hinges and latch, farm courtyard

DW-34 Weathered wood double doors with rough-sawn vertical planks and painted diagonal planks

DW-35 Weathered whitewashed wood-plank double doors, concrete-block shed

DW-36 Rustic wood-plank door with single brace, wrought-iron hardware, and two-paneled transom window; cambered arch; 16th- or 17th-c. England

BATTENED DOORS

DW-37 Trompe l'oeil wood-grained two-paneled double doors, dimensional flush molding; segmental arch

DW-38 Six-panel American Colonial–style door with flush molding, painted ornament on transom, and double-hung side lights

DW-39 Three-panel double doors with painted panels and painted carved ornament; segmental arch transom, Bali

DW-40 Two-panel double doors with raised panels, carved side panels, and pierced carved transom, all with metallic paint

PAINTED DOORS

DW-41 Painted paneled door with pentagonal light in top panel, brass letter slot, in brick entry with jack arch

DW-42 Door with painted panels and grille of turned spindles; stucco adobe doorway with exposed timber lintel, American Southwestern mission

DW-43 Weathered painted wood batten door with iron strap hinges

DW-44 Weathered double doors with painted panels; doorway recessed in stucco reveal with exposed timber lintel

PAINTED DOORS

DW-45 Brass three-paneled double doors, panels with lights and framed with molding; louvered brass transom panel

DW-46 Stainless steel double doors with full glass in circular muntins or grille

DW-47 Aluminum-clad revolving door with full glass

DW-48 Cast-bronze paneled hinged and revolving doors; pierced transom grille

METAL DOORS

DW-49 Brass double doors; full glass with radial muntins or grille; brass doorframe; Art Deco commercial building

DW-50 Brass double doors; full glass behind ornate brass grille; brass panels flanking doorframe

DW-51 Frameless glass double doors set in glass-block wall

DW-52 Metal-clad door with "quilted" panels; brick surround with rowlock course above door opening

DW-53 Rolling galvanized-metal security door with graffiti

DW-54 Weathering-steel garage doors with textured glass lights, modern house

METAL DOORS

DW-55 Welded and painted metal collage applied to door and frame, with textured metal threshold

DW-56 Painted metal door with stainless steel hardware; brushed stainless steel doorframe with transom light

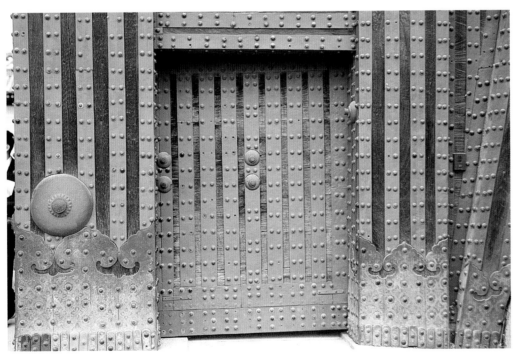

DW-57 Iron door inset in gate wall; bases of adjacent reveals clad in decorative metal work; 16th-c. Japanese castle

METAL DOORS

DW-58 Full glass double doors in stainless steel frame with three-light transom in recessed entryway; stone surround and steps, modern commercial building

DW-59 Brushed aluminum door with two lights in metal frame with transom light, modern apartment house

DW-60 Enamel-painted aluminum screen door with scrollwork and palm ornament

DW-61 Stainless steel door with single light and transom light; frame flanked by shutters, modern doorway in older urban building

METAL DOORS

DW-62 Oval transom light over wood paneled doors with single lights; doorframe flanked by Doric pilasters and entablature, 19th-c. apartment house

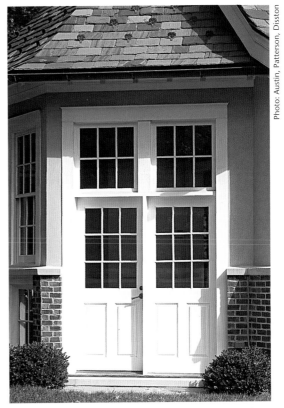

DW-63 Six-light double transom panels over nine-light painted wood double doors with center post, traditional house

DW-64 Side lights flanking twelve-light painted wood paneled door; gauged-brick jack arch in fieldstone wall; American colonial village building

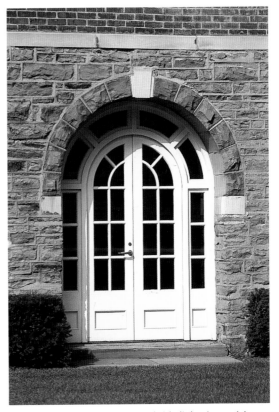

DW-65 Wood double doors and side lights in semicircular doorway; stone arch with keystone and imposts

TRANSOM LIGHTS & SIDE LIGHTS

DW-66 Painted wood doorway with eight-light transom panel over three-light side lights and single-light paneled door, commercial building

DW-67 Full glass double doors and side lights with three-light transom, modern house

DW-68 Full glass wood double doors and double side lights, modern house

DW-69 Paneled double doors with octagonal lights with leaded glass transom in cambered arch; letter slot; fluted pilasters; crown molding

DW-70 Paneled double doors and side lights with lancet-shaped lights and twelve-light transom; letter slot; Ionic-style pilasters and entablature

DW-71 Single-light door and side lights in rustic wood with curved timber eyebrow lintel

DW-72 Ornate arched entry with Corinthian capitals on engaged columns, fanlight, archivolt, cartouche keystone, and scrolled pediment

DW-73 Classical-style marble entry with steps, Corinthian columns and entablature, and pediment with block modillions

DW-74 Neoclassical entry with pairs of Ionic engaged columns supporting dentil entablature, eight-paneled double doors, bat-wing fanlight

DW-75 Stone segmental arch with carved wood double doors; keystone and corbels supporting a balcony, Parisian apartment house

DW-76 Pointed arch in banded stone over carved stone transom panel with bull's eye window; two-paneled single-light double doors, brick church

DW-77 Segmental arch with molded imposts over painted plank door; skull ornament in stucco surround, 19th-c. American Southwestern mission

Photo: Lockwood-Mathews Mansion-Museum

DW-78 Victorian conservatory entry: painted wood four-light door and transom light with etched glass; wood pilasters and crown molding; stone base

DW-79 Marble entry with diamond band, Florentine arch, and gauged-block jack arch over carved wood double doors, 16th-c. Italian church

DW-80 Door hood: arch with ornate pilasters, carved paneled doors, twelve-light transom panel; 19th-c. building

DW-81 Tuscan-style painted wood columns and entablature with pediment porch, paneled door, diamond side lights, traditional house

DW-82 Half-timber–style stucco and painted wood porte-cochère with eyebrow lintel over window, variegated Vermont slate roof

DW-83 Neoclassical pedimented door hood over pilasters and arched doorframe; wood panel door with fanlight

Photo: Austin, Patterson, Disston

DW-84 Door hood over engaged columns and double doors with diamond muntins, traditional house

DW-85 Crown molding door hood on cut brackets over paneled door with side lights, 19th-c. American house

DW-86 Arched entry with crown molding and pilasters around paneled door, side lights, and fanlight, 18th-c. American house

DW-87 Southwestern-mission–style entry with decorative belfry and profiled door surround

DW-88 Traditional Japanese entry with lattice screen under gable

DW-89 Traditional Japanese post-and-beam–style entry with extended eaves, double flush doors, full glass side lights and lattice gates, modern house

DW-90 Spanish-colonial–style recessed door in segmental arch framed with decorated glazed tiles on stucco wall; Mexican tile steps

DW-91 Door hood over arched doorway framed with wrought-iron filigree band; metal door with grille over full glass, modern house

DW-92 Spanish-colonial–style hotel entry with recessed wood gate under cambered arch

DW-93 Recessed entry with ornate horseshoe arch and steps

DW-94 Patio entry to stucco modern beach house: natural wood door with full glass

DW-95 Courtyard entry to modern house: door hood over natural wood paneled door with wood grille

DW-96 Traditional Japanese entry: double wood doors and stone steps

DW-97 Portico of metal-framed glass panels, modern commercial building

DW-98 Art Deco–style hotel entrance: steps flanked by decorated ceramic piers

DW-99 Grille-covered door and side lights with pilasters, modern commercial building

DW-100 Side entrance clad with stainless steel panels, modern concert hall

DW-101 Entry with large colored glass window and overhead lighted glass panels, modern commercial building

DW-102 Covered entryway: stainless steel double doors with full glass set in glass-paneled wall; masonry surround, modern commercial building

DW-103 Painted metal double doors flanked by side lights, stainless steel panels, and window wall

DW-104 Rustic stone cambered arch entry with wood battened door

DW-105 Weathered entry with wood molding, transom panel, and painted paneled door

DW-106 Café entry in ruins: wood-paneled double doors with lights flanked by wood-framed windows

DW-107 Entrance to temple courtyard: stone steps and carved surround with grotesque, Bali

DW-108 Chinese garden moon gate

DW-109 Garden entrance with wood-paneled doors in a stucco wall

DW-110 Unfinished-wood entry gate of alternating notched square stock and roughly dressed timber posts attached to horizontal battens

DW-111 Cast-bronze ornamented gate in stone wall

DW-112 Rustic garden gate of vertical branches attached to horizontal battens

DW-113 Sliding wood-lattice gate between roughly dressed timber posts, entrance to Japanese garden

GATES

DW-114 Wrought-iron gate recessed in wall

DW-115 Metal double gate with open bars and fan-shaped top panel in rustic stone arch with imposts on engaged columns

DW-116 Double bronze gates to mausoleum

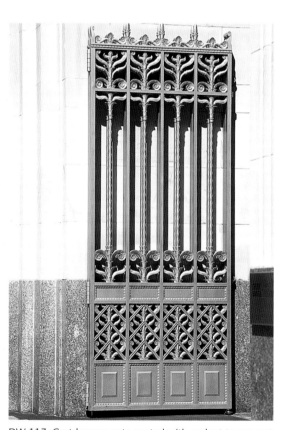

DW-117 Cast-bronze gate coated with sealant to prevent patination, commercial building

GATES

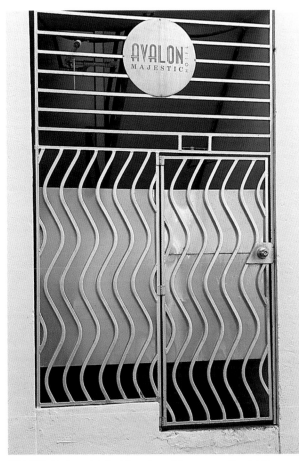

DW-118 Cast-metal double gates with upper grille, Art Deco hotel

DW-119 Entry gate of framed metal panels with brushed directional pattern in open rectangular frame, modern house

DW-120 Entry gate of cast metal in concentric rings, modern house

GATES

DW-121 Cast naturally patinated bronze door handle
with latch and lock

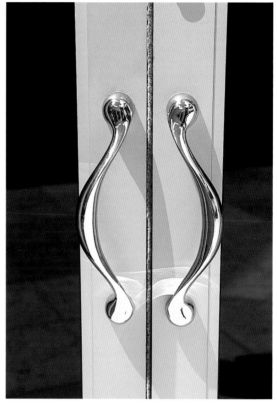

DW-122 Polished stainless steel modern door handles on
metal double door

DW-123 Traditional Japanese bronze and iron hardware
and door pull

DW-124 Cast-iron and brass door-pulls

DW-125 Decorative brass studs, grilles, and plates

DW-126 Polished bronze door knocker

CEILINGS & ROOFS

CR-1 Vaulted ceiling of porte-cochère, 19th-c. carriage entrance

CR-2 Roughly hewn exposed rafters anchored in adobe wall and covered with rough-sawn planks; 18th-c. American Southwestern mission

CR-3 Grass thatch roof showing connection between thatching and structure

CR-4 Exposed ceiling beams: painted steel frame and corrugated steel decking, modern house

CR-5 Woven split bamboo behind roughly hewn rafters, Indonesian pavilion

CR-6 Exposed select-fir framing in residential common room

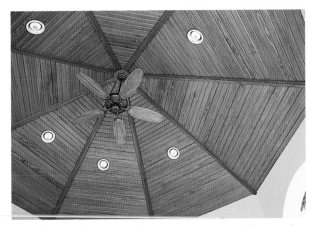

CR-7 Octagonal tongue-and-groove pool-house ceiling, modern house

CR-8 Painted barrel ceiling with tongue-and-groove between exposed ribs, modern house

CR-9 Plaster vaulted ceiling, traditional house

CEILINGS

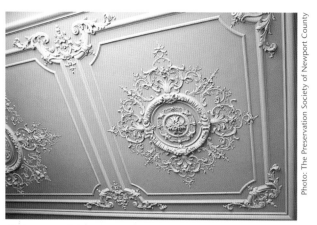

CR-10 Bas-relief ornamented ceiling panel, 19th-c. American mansion

Photo: The Preservation Society of Newport County

CR-11 Painted coffered ceiling, modern residential kitchen

Photo: Austin, Patterson, Disston

CR-12 Ceiling with decoratively painted coffers in an interlocking pattern, 19th-c. American mansion

Photo: Lockwood-Mathews Mansion Museum

CR-13 Ceiling of contrasting colored enameled panels in Art Deco design on portico

CR-14 Antique-chestnut coffered ceiling, residential library

Photo: Austin, Patterson, Disston

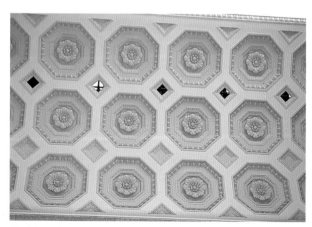

CR-15 Coffered ceiling with classically ornamented octagonal coffers

CR-16 Suspended atrium ceiling with interlocking "egg-crate" units, modern commercial building

CR-17 Elliptical atrium of metal-framed glass with pedestrian bridges, modern commercial building

CR-18 Metal-framed glass atrium ceiling, modern commercial building

CR-19 Metal-framed glass atrium ceiling, modern commercial building

CR-20 Glazed dome and adjacent vault, 19th-c. Italian building

Photo: Guy Gurney

CEILINGS

CR-21 Anodized aluminum or coated sheet steel with batten seams, modern commercial building

CR-22 Zinc or copper with flat seams, modern commercial building

CR-23 Copper shingles on curved hipped roof

CR-24 Zinc or copper flat seam, traditional Japanese roof

CR-25 Anodized aluminum awning, modern commercial building

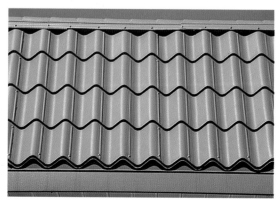

CR-26 Enameled corrugated metal imitating mission tile

METAL ROOFS

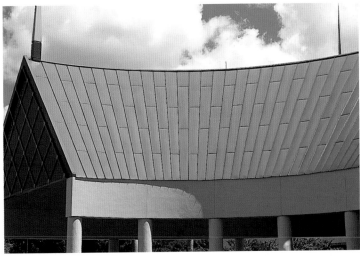

CR-27 Anodized aluminum or coated sheet steel with standing seams, curved gable roof, modern commercial building

CR-28 Sheet-metal shingles with flat seams on roof and dormers; pipe-style snow guard on lower edge

CR-29 Sheet metal with batten seams on gambrel roof and dormers, 19th-c. French apartment house

METAL ROOFS

CR-30 Anodized aluminum or coated sheet steel with standing seams, variation of hipped roof, modern house

CR-31 Anodized aluminum or coated sheet steel with a variety of flat and batten seams on roof and gable wall, modern commercial building

CR-32 Quilted sheet metal on dome roof of corner turret with flashing at juncture of dome and wall

CR-33 Sheet metal with standing seams on conical turret roof; hipped roof and hipped roof dormer, 19th-c. château-style hotel

METAL ROOFS

CR-34 Copper (top) and other varieties of sheet metal with batten and standing seams on hipped and conical roofs, 19th-c. château-style mixed-use buildings

CR-35 Copper with standing seams, hipped roof with cresting and arched roof dormer; copper cladding and molding on walls

CR-36 Sheet metal with standing seams on gable roof and glazed monitors, modern commercial building

CR-37 Weathered corrugated metal roofs with flared gable on barn and domed roof on silo

CR-38 Weathered corrugated metal barn roof with pyramidal roof on monitor

CR-39 Standing seams with hipped roof dormers

METAL ROOFS

CR-40 Weathered terracotta pantile with antefix at end of ridge tiles on hip, Balinese house

CR-41 New and weathered terracotta mission tiles. Top to bottom: shed roof; gable roof, half-cone roof

CR-42 Traditional Japanese tiles. Left: *hogawara*; right: *kawara*

CR-43 Weathered terracotta mission and flat tiles on shed roof

Photo: Duane Langenwalter

CR-44 Polychrome glazed ceramic end-tiles, Chinese roof

CR-45 Terracotta pantiles on hipped roof with ridge tiles on hip

CR-46 Weathered terracotta tiles on pyramidal roof

CR-47 Cast concrete pantiles on hipped roof with concrete ridge tiles on hip

CR-48 Japanese *kawara* tiles with ornamental tile antefixes

TILE ROOFS

CR-49 Flat multicolored shingle tiles with hipped roof dormers, 20th-c. American house

Photo: Guy Gurney

CR-50 Tile rooftops, Adriatic coastal village

CR-51 Detail of mission tiles at junction of gable and main roof

CR-52 Weathered flat shingle tiles with gabled roof dormer

CR-53 Flat shingle tiles on convex curved roof with copper molding, 19th-c. mixed-use building

TILE ROOFS

CR-54 Flat shingle terracotta tiles on gable roof with decorative ridge tiles, 19th-c. English house

CR-55 Multicolored mission tiles on hipped roof with shed roof over window, 20th-c. American house

CR-56 Terracotta pantiles with ridge ornament on variation of hipped roof, Balinese house

CR-57 Mission-tile roof with idiosyncratic gable and facade clad in scalloped tile shingles, 20th-c. American house

TILE ROOFS

CR-58 Variegated slate roofing on hipped roof with pyramidal wall dormer, American house

CR-59 Scalloped slate roofing in banded polychrome patterns around pedimented dormer

CR-60 Rectangular slate roofing in polychrome diaper pattern

CR-61 Variegated Vermont slate roofing with snow guards

CR-62 Scalloped slate roofing in banded pattern with inset stars

CR-63 Variegated slate with eyebrow dormer

Photo: Austin, Patterson, Disston

CR-64 Scalloped and diamond-shaped painted wood shingles

CR-65 Alaskan yellow cedar shingles; roof valley at intersection of gables; traditional American house.

CR-66 Split bamboo shingles on gabled roof, Indonesian house

CR-67 Wood shingles on hipped roof with antefix, Balinese shrine

CR-68 Asphalt shingles on roof with arched wall dormers

CR-69 Wood shingles on hipped roof with contrasting shingles along hip

Photo: Austin, Patterson, Disston

CR-70 Trimmed thatch on concrete-block building, Bali

CR-71 Palm-frond thatch, Balinese pavilion

CR-72 Underside of traditional palm thatched pavilion

CR-73 Scalloped roof ridge on traditional English thatched house

CR-74 Detail of thatching around gable, English barn

CR-75 Thatched roof on house, Latin America

Photo: Meredith Barchat

THATCHED ROOFS

CR-76 Wall dormer with jerkinhead roof

CR-77 Half-timber–style gable wall with tile roof, 20th-c. American house

Photo: Guy Gurney

CR-78 Pierced gingerbread-style gable and bargeboard ornament, Caribbean house

CR-79 Gable wall with carved half-timber–style bargeboard, 19th-c. American house

CR-80 Wall dormer with decorated bargeboard, American clapboard and shingle house

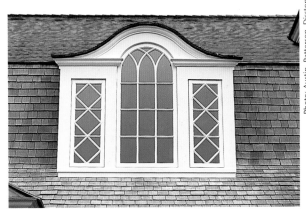

CR-81 Roof dormer with Palladian window

CR-82 Double roof dormers clad with slate shingles

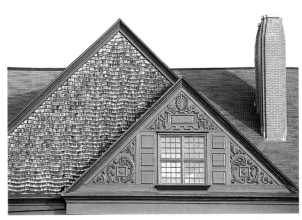

CR-83 Wall dormers. Left: shingle-clad; right: wood with carved ornament, American house

CR-84 Wood gable with lattice; ceramic tiles on gable roof and adjoining shed roof (bottom), Japanese temple

CR-85 Double wall dormers with gingerbread-style decorated bargeboard, 19th-c. American stone house

GABLES & DORMERS

CR-86 Shingled roof dormer above flared eave covering porch; stone gable-end wall

CR-87 Dormer with hipped roof on jerkinhead tile roof with scalloped terra-cotta tiles, gable-end wall

CR-88 Gable-end wall with new flush board siding above weathered siding; glazed monitor with pyramidal roof

GABLES & DORMERS

CR-89 Wall dormer on painted wood roof

CR-90 Three-sided roof dormer with windows and wood beam spanning gable roof, Arts and Crafts cedar-shingle house

CR-91 Hipped gable roof dormer; dormer and roof clad with pantiles

CR-92 Gabled wall dormer with Palladian window

CR-93 Pedimented gable roof dormer and shed-roof dormer

CR-94 Idiosyncratic half-timber gable, 16th-c. English house

CR-95 Half-timber wall gables with scalloped bargeboard flanking shed roof and flashing in roof valleys

Photo: Austin, Patterson, Disston

CR-96 Gable-end wall of flared gambrel roof with white cedar shingles; corbelled tie spanning gable

CR-97 Three hipped-roof dormers and a gabled wall dormer; slate cladding on roof dormers and roofs

CR-98 Segmental-arch roof dormers on mansard roof with metal shingles

CR-99 Flat-roofed wall dormers on metal roof

CR-100 Four flared-gable roof dormers above flared pyramidal roof dormers on metal hipped roof

CR-101 Shed-roof dormer on metal hipped roof with standing seams, modern house

CR-102 Hipped-roof dormers on metal hipped roof with pipe snow guards, modern apartment house

CR-103 Gable-roof dormers with deep eaves

CR-104 Shed-roof dormers on gambrel roof

CR-105 Cantilevered eave over wood structure, traditional Japanese pagoda

CR-106 Profiled eave brackets

CR-107 Wood eave brackets supporting mission-tile hipped roof, American Southwestern mission–style house

CR-108 Profiled eave brackets on modern Mediterranean-style house

CR-109 Overhangs of multileveled flat roofs, modern house

CR-110 Semidetached extension of metal roof connected to facade by Z-shaped brackets, modern commercial building

CR-111 Eaves of hipped roof on notched cross-beams, Arts and Crafts house

CR-112 Metal and wood gable with eave acting as door hood, modern beach house

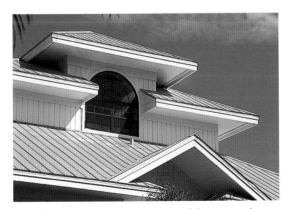

CR-113 Multiple eaves on hipped roof dormers and gable-wall dormers

CR-114 Eave of shed roof connected to balcony to shelter courtyard walkway, traditional Japanese house

CEILINGS & ROOFS

CR-115 Hipped, copper with standing seams; hipped-roof dormers (left) and pedimented wall dormer (right)

CR-116 Parapeted gable with hipped-roof dormers (left), hipped roof with hip dormers (right), and flared mansard with hip dormers (top), all sheet metal

Photo: Roger Bartels Architects, Dobyan & Dobyan Builders

CR-117 Flared-gable shingle roof with shed dormer and shed bay window

CR-118 Mansard with row of shed dormers (right) and alternating gable and shed dormers (left)

CR-119 Left: gable with gable monitor and cupola; right: pyramid roof with weather-vane

ROOF TYPES

298

CR-120 Left: gable with roof dormers, metal with flat seam; right: gable with hipped-roof dormers, wood shingle; flashing in roof valley

CR-121 Shingled saltbox

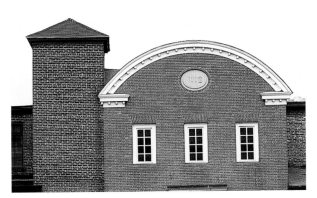

CR-122 Compass roof, fascia with modillions

CR-123 Half-timbered gable, with surface arch

CR-124 Steep half-timbered gable with shed dormer

CR-125 Half-timbered gable

CR-126 Slate gable roof and gabled roof dormer with bay

CR-127 Half-timber–style cross gable with variegated slate roofing

CR-128 Octagonal painted standing-seam metal roof with widow's walk and gabled roof dormer

CR-129 Flared gambrel, soffit with modillions

ROOF TYPES

CR-130 Idiosyncratic metal roof with standing seams

CR-131 Composite dome, metal with standing-seam

CR-132 Pyramidal metal roof

CR-133 Pyramidal octagonal roof on turret, cross-gable dormers

ROOF TYPES

CR-134 Ogee slate roof adjacent to gable roof, both with metal ridge ornamentation

CR-135 Pagoda

CR-136 Thatched gable on hipped roof, Japanese temple

CR-137 Hipped roofs: open shingled (left); metal with standing seams (right)

CR-138 Shed and flat roofs, painted metal, with batten seams

CR-139 Hipped roof with octagonal cupolas, metal with standing seams

ROOF TYPES

R-140 Flat, punctured roof with projecting eave and palm trees growing through concrete canopy

CR-141 Cantilevered fabric awning springing from freestanding stucco wall and ceiling, outdoor public space

CR-142 Shed-roofed entry with revealed rafters, braces, and joists

ROOF TYPES

CR-143 Brick-pilaster chimneys: spiral (left); banded (right)

CR-144 Coursed-rubble chimney

CR-145 Brick chimneys with hipped chimney hoods

CR-146 Engaged rectangular chimney stack

Photo: Guy Gurney

CR-147 Stucco chimney

CR-148 Stucco-over-brick chimney with pyramidal hood

CR-149 Brick chimney

CR-150 Chimney: coursed-ashlar buttress and random ashlar stonework, herringbone brick

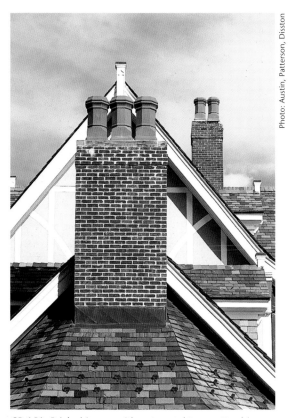

Photo: Austin, Patterson, Disston

CR-151 Brick chimney with octagonal terracotta chimney pots

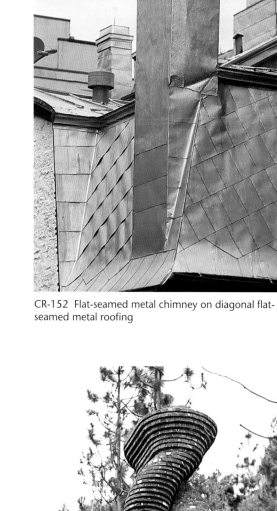

CR-152 Flat-seamed metal chimney on diagonal flat-seamed metal roofing

CR-153 Coursed-rubble chimney

CR-154 Spiral brick chimney pot

CHIMNEYS

CR-155 Detail of wood and bamboo gutter and rain-water head, Japan

CR-156 Metal decorated gutter, rainwater head, and drainpipe

CR-157 Metal gutter, drainpipe, and rainwater head

CR-158 Copper drainpipe and rainwater head

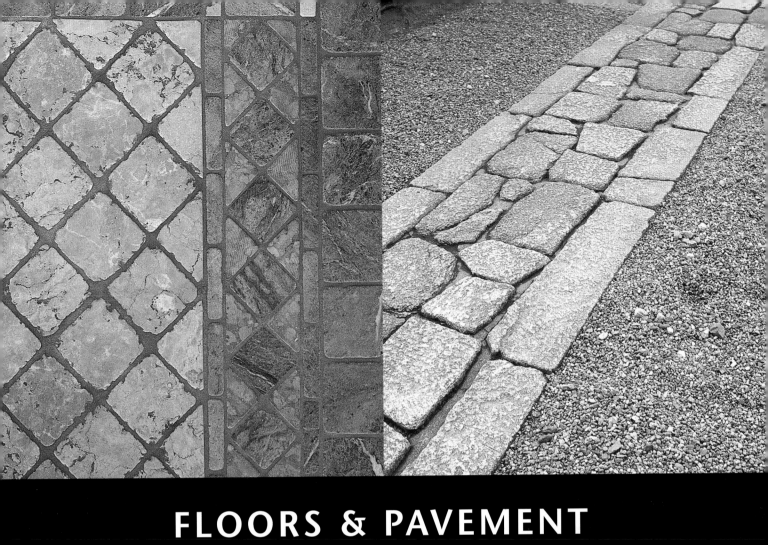

FLOORS & PAVEMENT

FP-1 Decking: two varieties of wood in circular design

FP-2 Dressed logs with center-sawn planks and wood-peg construction, rustic garden bridge

FP-3 Wood decking: pool surround with inset circle

FP-4 Ash flooring and Chinese granite tile, residential foyer

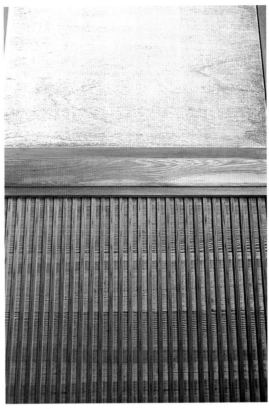

FP-5 Top to bottom: framed-wood raised floor; door sill; closely spaced narrow strips of wood over sawn planks

FP-6 Canadian elm flooring with cherry cabinetwork

FP-7 Ash flooring and steps with rounded nosing in balcony hallway

FP-8 Grooved weather-treated wood decking alternating with metal grates, urban public space

FP-9 Split-bamboo deck

FP-10 Wood planks with concrete surround, courtyard walkway

FP-11 Wood deck around reflecting pool (at left)

Photo: Austin, Patterson, Disston

FP-12 Ipe-wood deck in flagstone walk; painted mahogany benches

Photo: The Preservation Society of Newport County

FP-13 Marble parquet in framed hexagon pattern in foyer

FP-14 Marble and fossil-stone parquet in circular design, pavilion floor

Photo: Lockwood-Mathews Mansion Museum

FP-15 Marble parquet in polychrome geometric pattern in foyer

FP-16 Marble parquet in circular radiating design in foyer

FP-17 Marble parquet in polychrome geometric pattern, interior of modern commercial building

FP-18 Travertine and marble parquet in geometric pattern with marble polychrome band in foyer

FP-19 Travertine paving stone in banded pattern, urban public space

FP-20 Dimension fieldstone in running bond with soldier-course border and stone gutter, garden walkway

FP-21 Paving stones set in concrete in running bond with soldier-course border adjacent to natural rock wall, garden path

FP-22 Dimension slate in geometric pattern, garden path

STONE FLOORS & PAVEMENT

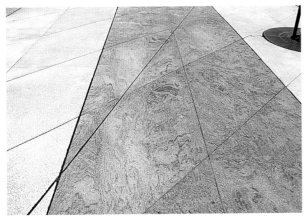

FP-23 Dark and light dimension-granite paving stone in diagonal design, urban public space

FP-24 Grouted squared bluestone in various colors, sidewalk

FP-25 Squared and roughly squared textured paving stones on curved walkway, urban public space

FP-26 Stone stairway divided by stone ramps, urban public space

FP-27 Textured dimension paving stone with straight joints (top), and running bond (bottom), metal grates, and river rocks in courtyard of modern commercial building

FP-28 Roughly squared paving stone in random-ashlar pattern on sidewalk

FP-29 Roughly squared paving stone in random-ashlar pattern with moss on sidewalk

FP-30 Left to right: paving stone in running bond; natural stones; concrete

FP-31 Paving stone on street

FP-32 Weathered paving stone on street

FP-33 Tumbled paving stone, courtyard of modern commercial building

FP-34 Paving stone in ramp-like steps, entry of modern commercial building

FP-35 Jumbo cobblestones in intersecting running bonds on an ancient street

FP-36 Paving stone in fan pattern with drain cover

STONE FLOORS & PAVEMENT

FP-37 Paving stone in running bond (left), with split fieldstones around split bolders; border of roughly squared paving stone

FP-38 Uncoursed fieldstone used as divider in running-bond brick driveway, Arts and Crafts residence

FP-39 Random round cobbles set in concrete, garden path

STONE FLOORS & PAVEMENT

318

FP-40 Variegated flagstone in mosaic pattern, urban public space

FP-41 Split, polished boulders between squared and textured paving stones in running bond, urban public space

FP-42 Small, split, polished fieldstones set in concrete and bordering light-colored flagstone, forming steps

FP-43 Large round boulders surrounded by split natural stones, both set in concrete, garden path

FP-44 Roughly squared, textured dimension stone in banded pattern, garden walk

FP-45 Variegated flagstone; flexible paving, patio floor

FP-46 Steps made from roughly squared split, polished fieldstone set in concrete. Bottom left: bamboo drain cover

STONE FLOORS & PAVEMENT

FP-47 Flagstone path in rock garden

FP-48 Squared granite blocks with split-stone inset on garden path

FP-49 Cylindrical steppingstones in pond, Japanese garden

FP-50 Roughly squared paving stone in diamond pattern with border, garden path

STONE FLOORS & PAVEMENT

Photo: Austin, Patterson, Disston

FP-51 Hammered limestone and beach pebbles with drain around concrete tub, bathhouse

FP-52 Gravel around natural and squared stone, Japanese Zen garden

FP-53 Paving stone made from river stone and cement, Indonesian courtyard

FP-54 Detail of rock garden with beach pebbles between large gravel (bottom) and fine raked gravel (top)

STONE FLOORS & PAVEMENT

FP-55 Steppingstones surrounded by gravel, residential entryway

Photo: Austin, Patterson, Disston

FP-56 Left to right: oiled stone gravel on asphalt paving; mortared running-bond cobblestones; New York bluestone step, residential driveway

FP-57 Beach pebbles bordered by moss and concrete or stone

STONE FLOORS & PAVEMENT

Photo: Austin, Patterson, Disston

FP-58 Brick pavers in running bond bordered by soldier courses intersecting pebble path; flexible paving, garden walk

FP-59 Running-bond variations in mortared brick paving, residential driveway

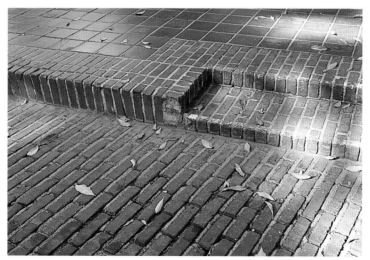

FP-60 Top to bottom: Mexican paving tile, straight-joint installation; mortared brick pavement and steps in running bond; soldier-course brick curb, residential entry

BRICK PAVEMENT

FP-61 Belgian-blend brick in running bond; soldier-course border and facing of mahogany decking, residential patio

FP-62 Brick pavers in stack bond alternating with wood planks and large-aggregate concrete, urban public space

FP-63 Stone curb and Roman brick in herringbone pattern on ancient sidewalk

FP-64 Mortared brick in running bond, bordered by soldier courses in straight and curved paths intersecting with pebble path and grass, garden walk

BRICK PAVEMENT

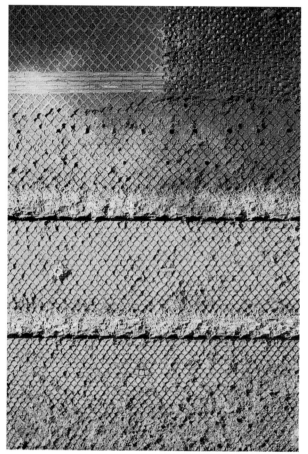

FP-65 Overhead view of weathered brick paving, ancient Roman ruins

FP-66 Overhead view of weathered brick and tile paving, ancient Roman ruins

FP-67 Paving brick in herringbone pattern; flexible paving

BRICK PAVEMENT

FP-68 Pebbles set in concrete in diaper pattern with stone border

FP-69 Pre-cast paving blocks of light-colored exposed aggregate in a field of dark-colored exposed aggregate

FP-70 Exposed aggregate with terracotta tile insets on steps and floor in entryway. Aggregate applied, not revealed by washing

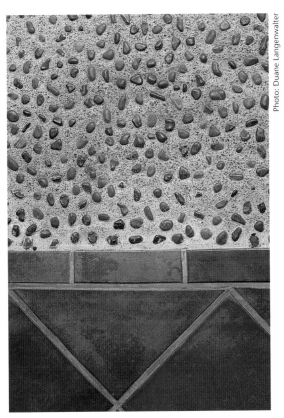

FP-71 Exposed aggregate with tile border. Aggregate applied, not revealed by washing

Photo: Duane Langenwalter

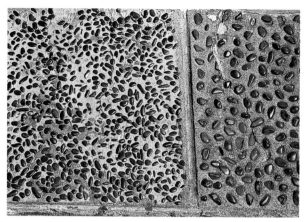

FP-72 Adjacent squares of medium (left) and large (right) exposed aggregate. Aggregate applied, not revealed by washing

FP-73 Squares of exposed aggregate (possibly pre-cast) separated by metal or concrete grid in courtyard of modern commercial building

FP-74 Pea-sized gravel aggregate (right) next to randomly shaped and placed tile

FP-75 Curved steps faced with large exposed aggregate. Aggregate applied, not revealed by washing

FP-76 Pea-sized gravel aggregate inset with rows of rocks and bordered by small split, polished fieldstone set in concrete

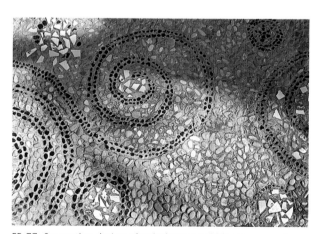

FP-77 Serpentine design of polychrome pebbles in exposed aggregate

FP-78 Top to bottom: circle diaper pattern stamped in concrete; metal grate drain cover; pre-cast polychrome concrete pavers in herringbone pattern

FP-79 Concrete textured to resemble rough wood planks, possibly cast-in-place, with texture produced by forming materials

FP-80 Cast-in-place concrete stamped with pattern of stone paving and footprint in sidewalk

FP-81 Polychrome asphalt pattern; flexible paving, urban public space

FP-82 Pre-cast concrete pavers; double soldier course in straight-joint-course field; flexible paving, urban public space

FP-83 Polychrome pre-cast concrete textured pavers: mosaic area (top) bordered by straight-joint border, urban public space

FP-84 Polychrome pre-cast concrete pavers in herringbone and banded patterns, urban street

FP-85 Polychrome pre-cast concrete pavers in geometric pattern with drain, urban public space

FP-86 Tumbled pre-cast concrete pavers in random-ashlar pattern; flexible paving (left) bordered by terracotta tile and drain grate, urban public space

FP-87 Random-shaped ceramic and stone tiles in mosaic pattern surrounded by random-ashlar pavers, urban public space

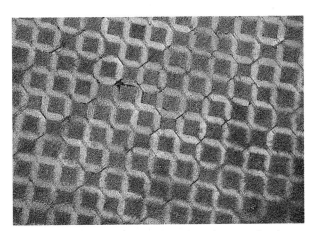

FP-88 Concrete screen-wall blocks set into the ground and planted with grass in patio

FP-89 Flexible paving: concrete pavers in herringbone pattern (top), with border course; tumbled random-size concrete pavers in running bond (bottom), urban public space

FP-90 Terrazzo in border and star design, hotel entryway

FP-91 Decorated glazed ceramic tiles surrounded by stone in running bond, commercial entry

FP-92 Round porcelain tile mosaic in hexagon pattern with square border tiles, commercial entry

FP-93 Square stone tile mosaic in neoclassical design and Greek-key border, commercial entry

FP-94 Trapezoidal concrete pavers inlaid with ceramic tiles and pebbles, patio

FP-95 Paving tiles in octagonal border with central ornament

FP-96 Square decorated glazed tile in a field of straight-jointed ceramic tiles, modern commercial entry

FP-97 Irregular pieces of ceramic tile set in raised concrete, patio

FP-98 Polychrome glazed terracotta tile in geometric pattern

FP-99 Mexican paving tiles, straight-jointed, and inset with small decorated glazed tiles in diaper pattern, vertical-joint border (right)

FP-100 Squares of pre-grouted stone mosaic tiles in checker design with dark mosaic grid outline squares, commercial entry

FP-101 Square and triangular ceramic tiles set in exposed-aggregate field in geometric and random patterns, entryway

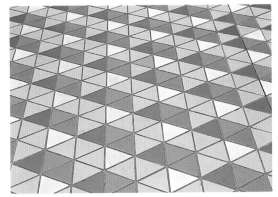

FP-102 Triangular ceramic tiles in geometric pattern, urban public space

FP-103 Shards of decorated ceramic plates used as tesserae in mosaic steppingstone, residential entryway

FP-104 Random-shaped tile pieces used as tesserae in mosaic grid design set in concrete

FP-105 Decorated glazed tile, straight-jointed, forming diaper patterns, and a running-repeat border

FP-106 Mosaic floor with lettering, logo, and decorative border, hotel entry

FP-107 Directional arrow set in safety paving with metal strip border, surrounded by pre-cast exposed aggregate, urban public space

FP-108 Metal safety-paving brads on flagstone set in concrete, urban public space

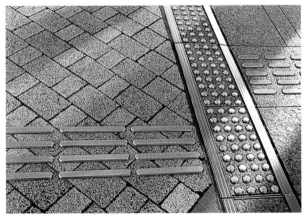

FP-109 Metal safety-paving brads and strips applied to granite pavers, urban public space

FP-110 Cast-iron manhole cover with decorative pattern and lettering

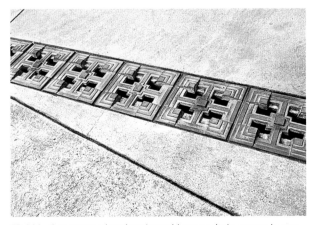

FP-111 Ornamented and patinated bronze drain covers in concrete driveway

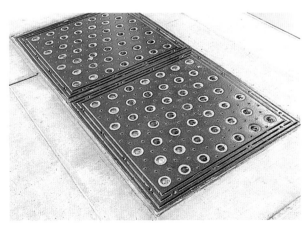

FP-112 Steel plates with colored glass insets, sidewalk loading lift cover

FP-113 Pre-cast exposed-aggregate drain grates in gutter beside a walkway, urban park

FP-114 Cast-iron manhole cover decorated with rosettes

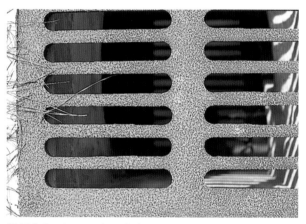

FP-115 Rusting cast-iron drain grate

FP-116 Expanded-metal sidewalk grate with applied steel footprints

FP-117 Steel drain grate inset into dimension paving stone and gravel with natural rock border

FP-118 Decorated cast-iron street plate inset into pavers

GLOSSARY

abacus. The square slab crowning a capital, directly under the architrave. It may be enriched with molding. CP-6.

acanthus. A leaf shape, from the plant of the same name, that forms the basis for an ornament used to enrich molding and to decorate Corinthian and Composite capitals. OM-12, GL-1.

adobe. (1) Unfired brick, often containing straw, dried in the sun. GL-2. (2) The structures made from adobe brick.

aggregate. Granular material mixed with cement to form concrete, mortar, pebble dash, or terrazzo. The size of the granules may vary from sand to pebbles and is determined by the requirements of the application. FP-72, GL-3.

American bond. *See* bond.

American order. A variation of the Corinthian order capital with acanthus leaves replaced by corn cobs, tobacco leaves, or other regional element. CP-24.

anchor iron. An exposed, often decorative, end piece of a steel rod that connects opposing brick walls and provides structural reinforcement by pulling in the walls. WA-174.

ancon. A wedge-shaped console. CP-141, GL-4.

angle capital. Ionic capital variation that resolves a corner column by angling four volutes at 45 degrees from their traditional orientation. CP-69.

angular capital. Ionic capital variation in which all four sides, eight volutes, are angled at 45 degrees from their traditional orientation. Also called Scamozzi capital. CP-6.

anta. The end of a wall treated as a pilaster. CP-83.

antefix. The upright ornament on the peak of a gable or eave or at the ends of a roof. CR-48.

anthemion. An ornament in the shape of a cluster of leaf-like forms radiating from a central point, often used as a running repeated ornament. OM-54.

antic. An ornament in a caricature human, animal, or floral form. OM-10.

annulet. A band encircling a column. CP-68.

arcade. A passageway formed by arches on the same plane supported by columns or piers. CP-135.

architectural terracotta. Fired clay used on facades and for architectural ornament. FA-61.

archivolt. A decorative band or molding around the face of an arch. CP-147.

architrave. (1) The bottom member of an entablature, the part closest to the column. OM-107. (2) A molding around a door or window. OM-53.

ashlar. A term describing stone that has been cut and squared and the surface finished. WA-67.

astragal. A half-round molding usually composed of a string of half-globe beads or bead-and-reel shapes. Also called bead molding. OM-66.

Attic. Column base composed of molding on a plinth, in this order from top to bottom: torus, scotia, torus, plinth. CP-34.

awning window. A window that swings or pivots open from the top of the frame, keeping a horizontal orientation. WI-39.

baldachin. A canopy-like structure, often supported by columns, used to give emphasis. OM-43.

band. An ornamental molding in low relief, often with a repeated motif. OM-1.

banded. A term describing a construction, such as a masonry wall or a column, with units of contrasting color, texture, or material in the coursing producing horizontal stripes. WA-70, CP-94.

bargeboard. A board, often decorated, under the eave of a gable, which seals the space between the roof and the wall. CR-79, GL-5.

base. (1) The part of a column between the bottom of the shaft and the pedestal, plinth, or ground. CP-34. (2) The bottom course of a masonry wall or the first horizontal member of a finished floor.

basket-weave. A pattern made by placing pairs of units perpendicular to adjacent pairs of similar units. WA-166.

batten door. A door built from vertical planks joined by visible top and bottom horizontal planks (battens). DW-24.

battered wall. A wall that inclines and is thicker at the base than at the top. WA-49.

bay window. A window that protrudes from the main structure of a building. WI-77.

bead-and-reel. Molding shaped in an alternating pattern of beads and convex elements (reels), often arranged as one bead to two reels. OM-64.

bead molding. A convex molding that is semicircular in section. WA-89. *See also* astragal.

beam. A horizontal structural element with vertical supports.

Belgian block. A rectangular stone block (usually granite) used for paving.

belt course. A horizontal band of masonry, timber, or molding of a building. WA-64.

blind. A term describing an architectural element that, for design purposes, mimics an opening such as a door or arch but is nonfunctional. GL-6.

block modillion. *See* modillion.

board-and-batten. Exterior siding made from adjacent vertical boards with the joints covered by narrow strips (battens) of the same material. WA-4.

bonder. *See* header.

bond. An arrangement of masonry units in a pattern that may be structural or purely decorative. Units that do not form a pattern are *random bond*. General patterns are *basket-weave, diagonal bond, herringbone, running bond, stack bond*. Patterns specific to brick are *common (American) bond, English bond, Flemish bond*. Stone patterns are *coursed* and *random ashlar, mosaic (cobweb), coursed* and *uncoursed rubble*. *See also* individual entries.

bow window. A bay window circular in plan view. *See* compass window.

brick. Rectangular masonry units formed of clay or shale, in a plastic state and then dried or fired. Brick nomenclature depends on the orientation of the unit: *header, sailor, shiner, soldier, stretcher, rowlock. See also* individual entries.

broken pediment. A pediment with a space at the top, usually a decorative shape and sometimes filled with an ornament. FA-113.

bull's-eye window. A round or oval window, also called oeil-de-beouf. WI-61, GL-7.

bush-hammered. A term describing a mechanically produced textured masonry finish varying from subtle to rough. WA-217.

camber. A term describing an arch or window with a shallow top curve. WA-288, CP-90.

GL-1 Acanthus

GL-2 Adobe

GL-3 Aggregate and pebble dash

GL-4 Ancon

GL-5 Bargeboard

GL-6 Blind

GL-7 Bull's eye window

cames. Cast-lead muntins, H-shaped in section, that hold small panes of glass in windows. WI-3.

cant-bay window. A bay window with sides angled in plan view. WI-77.

capital. The uppermost section of a column or pilaster. Types include: *Composite, Corinthian, Doric, Ionic. See* individual entries.

cap. The uppermost element within an architectural unit. WA-290.

cartouche. A self-contained ornamental unit, often in relief, framed, and with an inscription. GL-8.

casement. A window that swings open from the side of the window frame. WI-39, GL-9.

casing. The molding around a door or window opening covering the juncture of the wall and the jamb.

cavetto. Classically, a concave molding, quarter-round in section, with the upper part of the quarter-round extended; it is usually placed above a torus. Often used at the juncture of a ceiling and a wall. Also called cove molding. OM-54.

chimney hood. The cap of a chimney that protects the opening from the elements without interfering with the escape of smoke and gas. CR-145.

chimney pot. A vertical unit on top of the chimney that improves the draft. CR-151.

chimney stack. A group of structurally connected separate chimneys or flues. CR-151.

chinking. Material that fills the spaces between the logs in log-cabin construction. WA-29.

clapboard. An exterior siding of overlapping boards applied to the framing or cladding. WA-16.

classical order. *See* order.

cobble. A small, naturally smooth rock used for building and paving. WA-108.

cobblestone. A stone used in paving. It may be rectangular, or naturally rounded. FP-35.

cobweb bond. *See* mosaic bond.

coffered ceiling. A ceiling composed of a series of recessed panels surrounded by raised beams. CR-11.

column. A vertical, detached, usually structural element. In classical architecture, it is composed of a capital, shaft, and, usually, base. *See also* order. CP-70.

column base. The portion of a column directly below the shaft and resting on the pedestal. CP-34.

common (American) bond. A structural brick bond consisting of courses of stretchers with a course of headers at regular intervals, usually every sixth or seventh course. *See also* bonds. WA-153, GL-10.

compass roof. A convex curved roof. CR-122.

Composite order. The group of columns, capitals, and entablatures with capitals that combine the Corinthian acanthus leaf with Ionic volutes. Also called compound order. *See also* order. GL-11.

console. A scroll-shaped bracket with parallel sides that is attached to a wall and supports a horizontal element. *See also* ancon. OM-12.

coping. An angled cap that protects the top edge of a wall from the elements. WA-271.

corbel. A projection from a wall, sometimes stepped, that adds support to an arch or other architectural element. It may be solely decorative. WA-189.

Corinthian order. The group of columns, capitals, and entablatures characterized by a capital composed of acanthus leaves, and, usually, a fluted column. *See also* order. CP-10.

corner board. A vertical molding placed on the exterior corner of a clapboard-clad house. The siding

boards are butted to, or are under the corner board. WA-37.

cornice. (1) The uppermost part of a classical entablature. (2) The uppermost molding on an architectural unit—for example, molding on the top of a pediment. OM-42.

corona. The part of a cornice with a flat face and a soffit, supporting the crown molding. OM-103.

Cosmatesque, cosmati-work. Flat, polychrome, geometric ornament made from marble, stone, or glass. CP-60.

course. A horizontal row of shingles or masonry units.

coursed ashlar. Ashlar masonry laid out in courses of equal height; blocks of various sizes may be combined to make up the height of the course. WA-95.

coursed rubble. Fieldstone or roughly dressed stone, with or without mortar, assembled to give a effect of courses. *See also* bond. WA-56.

cove molding. *See* cavetto.

cresting. A decorative profile at the top of a roof, wall, or cornice. CR-35, GL-12.

crenel. An open space in a parapet wall. WA-196.

crossette. (1) A six-sided voussoir with a projection resting on the voussoir below. WA-112.
(2) A molding used as framing with a square protrusion at the corners resembling an ear. OM-55.

cross-gable. A gable parallel to the ridge. GL-13.

crown molding. The uppermost molding on a wall, entablature, or group of moldings. WI-125.

curtain wall. A nonstructural exterior wall that is attached to a load-bearing structure.

cut bracket. A flat support with a profile, often resembling a console. DW-85.

cyma. A molding in section composed of one concave curve and one convex curve. A *cyma recta* has the concave curve on the top portion of the molding. A *cyma reversa* has the concave curve on the bottom portion of the molding. Also called ogee and reverse ogee. OM-70.

deck roof. *See* flat roof.

dentil. A square or rectangular molding element that is repeated with regular spacing in a toothlike pattern called dentilation. OM-70.

diagonal bond. A decorative masonry pattern, that is a variation of running bond with the units set on a diagonal in relation to the edges of the area being covered. *See also* Bonds. FP-59.

diaper. A pattern that repeats on a diagonal. WA-198.

dimension stone. Natural building stone that has been cut and finished to specification. WA-68.

dog-tooth course. A horizontal course of bricks with units laid on a diagonal to the face of the wall so the corners protrude, forming a dimensional serrated band. WA-194.

door casing. The molding around a door, covering the door frame and its attachment to the wall.

door frame. The structure, attached to the wall and enclosing and supporting the door, made of two vertical members (door jambs) connected by a horizontal member (door head jamb), often covered by a casing.

door hood. An overhang above a door that shelters the entry. DW-84.

Doric order. The group of columns, capitals, and entablatures characterized by an undecorated capital and simply decorated entablature. The Greek variety usually has a fluted shaft with no base. In the Roman style, the shaft is usually not fluted but

GL-8 Cartouche

GL-9 Casement

GL-10 Common bond

GL-11 Composite order (capital)

GL-12 Cresting

GL-13 Cross-gable

has a base. OM-108, CP-79.

dormer. An enclosed structure projecting from the slope of a roof, usually with a window or louvered opening. Also called roof dormer. *See also* wall dormer. CR-100.

double-hung window. A two-sash window that opens and closes by vertically sliding on parallel guides in the window frame. If only one window opens, it is single-hung.

drywall. Stone laid without mortar. WA-81.

durex blocks. Roughly cubed, usually granite blocks used for paving. GL-14.

Dutch bond. *See* Flemish bond.

echinus. Convex projecting molding directly below the abacus. CP-18.

egg-and-dart. Ovolo molding with alternating egg-shaped and dart-shaped ornament. GL-15.

embrasure. A window opening, wider on the inside than on the outside, in a thick wall. Derived from fortification structures, it enabled a wider angle of defense. WI-121.

end gable. *See* gable.

engaged column. A column, curved in plan, partially buried in a wall. *See also* pilaster. CP-95.

English bond. A structural brick bond with a course of stretchers alternating with a course of headers. *See also* bond. WA-154.

entablature. (1) The decorative bands and molding that cover the horizontal area above columns. Classically, it is composed of an architrave, frieze, and cornice. CP-9, GL-16. (2) A horizontal crown member with architrave, frieze, and cornice. OM-75.

entasis. A subtle swelling given to the body of a tapered structure, usually the shaft of a column to counter the optical illusion of narrowing. CP-78.

exposed aggregate. A concrete finish achieved by washing away the outer skin of mortar before concrete has fully hardened, thereby exposing the aggregate, usually gravel size or larger. FP-73.

extrados. The outside of an archivolt. CP-154.

eyebrow dormer. A dormer with a window without defined sides. The roof curves up to accommodate the height of the window. CR-63.

facade. The exterior wall of a building intended to be the front, designated as a result of orientation to the street or by ornamental details. FA-59.

fanlight. A fixed semicircular window, often found over a door and often divided by radiating muntins or decorative linear elements. WI-96.

fascia. (1) The undecorated horizontal member in an entablature. OM-63. (2) Any flat horizontal member that projects from a wall.

fenestration. The placement and design of window groupings. WI-156.

festoon. An ornament based on a botanical garland that appears to be suspended from two or more points. OM-14.

fieldstone. Stone found on the ground (i.e., not quarried) that is a suitable size and shape for use as drywall or rubble masonry. WA-270.

fillet. (1) A flat raised band used as molding. CP-34. (2) The flat surface between column flutes.

finial. An ornament that caps an architectural element. OM-49.

fixed light. A window with one or more lights that do not open. WI-59.

flagstone. Thin slabs of stone used for wall veneer and paving. FP-45.

flared eave. An eave with a slope that changes as it reaches the edge of the roof. The area between the top pitch and the final pitch is a concave curve. CR-86.

flashing. Thin sheet metal applied to a joint vulnerable to water leakage—for example, at the juncture of a chimney and a roof. CR-99.

flat roof. A roof with no apparent pitch but often with a slight slope to allow for drainage. Also called deck or terrace roof. CR-138.

Flemish bond. A structural brick bond, each course consisting of alternate stretchers and headers, with the headers in alternate courses centered over the stretcher. *See also* bond. WA-157.

flexible paving. Pavement set on a bed of compacted sand and gravel rather than a rigid bed such as reinforced concrete. FP-58.

Florentine arch. An arch with intrados and extrados with different radii, so the archivolt is not a parallel band. CP-154.

fluting. Vertical channels on a column shaft. CP-38.

foil. One of the three or more segments that make up tracery ornament. Tracery is defined by the number of foils: trefoil, quatrefoil, cinquefoil, sexfoil. CP-170, GL-17.

foliation. Decoration or construction with botanical forms—for example, a Corinthian capital. GL-18.

French doors. Double casement windows that extend to the floor and may function as doors. GL-19.

frieze. (1) The middle element of a classical entablature. OM-84. (2) A belt course, sometimes decorative, immediately below a cornice. OM-60.

gable. The usually triangular upper portion of an exterior wall formed by the meeting of the slopes of a pitched roof. If the gable is parallel to the front of the building, it is a cross or front gable; if perpendicular, it is a side or end gable. CR-88.

gable-on-hip. A roof that is partially hipped with small gables at each end formed where the hips change pitch and then rise vertically to the ridge. CR-136.

gable roof. A common roof type with two slopes at the same pitch that intersect at the ridge, resulting in a triangular gable at each end. CR-124.

gable wall. The wall with the gable formed by a gable roof. CR-88.

gallet. A small filler stone inserted into joints in rubble or rough-cut stone walls. WA-73.

gambrel roof. A roof, not hipped, with multiple pitches on each side of the ridge. CR-129.

gargoyle. A figurative, often fantastical, architectural sculpture projecting from a building. OM-21.

gauged brick. Brick made to a specific shape to fit into arches, panels, or ornamental bands. WA-169.

glazed. A term describing (1) an opening filled with glass or (2) ceramic tile with a finish that has been fused to the body of the tile by heat.

Gothic cornice. A motif consisting of connected pointed, nonstructural arches. OM-88.

Greek key. A geometric ornament composed of repeated horizontal and vertical bars intersecting at right angles forming an interlocking, mazelike pattern. OM-55.

grotesque. An ornament formed by a composition of botanical and animal forms. DW-107.

guilloche. An ornamental band composed of a series of circles outlined by an interlocking plaited band. OM-100.

GL-14   Durex blocks

GL-15   Egg-and-dart

GL-16   Entablature

GL-17   Foil

GL-18   Foliation

GL-19   French doors

gutta (pl. guttae). Truncated-pyramid or cone-shaped ornament found under mutules and often below metopes; under metopes, the shape is flattened. OM-55, OM-108.

half-timber. (1) Timber-framed construction with the areas between the framing filled with brick, stucco, or some other material. WA-273. (2) A decorative style imitating half-timber construction. WA-42.

header. A masonry unit placed in the course with its smallest surface facing out and with its rectangular shape in a horizontal position. It may interlock with a structural wall behind. Also called bonder. WA-170.

herringbone. A pattern that results from laying rectangular units at a 45-degree angle with alternating rows reversing direction and interlocking with the previous row. *See also* bond. WA-266, FP-67.

hip. The angled side of a roof, where adjacent slopes meet. CR-47.

hipped roof. Roof with four slopes, usually with two pitches. Two opposing slopes meet at the ridge, and the remaining slopes intersect with the ends of the ridge, forming the hips. CR-115, GL-20.

honed. A term describing a smooth masonry finish with little or no gloss. WA-68.

impost. A block, often decorated, at an end of an arch, under the springer that distributes the thrust of the arch. OM-56.

infill. The material filling the frame of a timber-frame structure. WA-277.

intrados. The lower or inside curve of the voussoirs of an arch. CP-154.

Ionic order. The group of columns, columns, and entablatures characterized by a capital with twin volutes. CP-2.

jamb. The vertical part of the structural frame holding a door or window.

jamb-shaft. A small column or shaft set into the corner formed by the intersection of a door or window and the reveal of a wall. CP-68.

jetty. The overhang of an upper story over a lower story. WA-37.

jerkinhead. A roof only hipped for a part of its height, resulting in a truncated gable. CR-87.

keystone. The uppermost and last set masonry element in an arch, which locks the units together, usually wedge-shaped with side angles corresponding to the radius of the arch. WA-112.

knocked-down skip-trowel. A plaster or stucco finish produced by troweling over a partially set texture, leaving patches untouched. Also called Italian or California finish. WA-238.

lancet window. A tall, narrow, pointed-arched window. GL-21.

leaded glass. Pieces of glass, often colored, combined into a single window by means of lead or zinc muntins or cames. Also called leaded light.

leader head. *See* rainwater head.

light. (1) An opening that admits daylight. (2) A pane of window glass.

lintel. A horizontal support for an opening. CP-109.

mansard. A hipped roof with the slopes in two sets of planes, the top set more steeply sloped and usually with dormer windows in the lower set. GL-22.

mascaron. A caricature of a human face used as an architectural ornament. OM-9.

mason's miter. A method used for stone molding placed around a corner: the stone is not cut into mitered pieces and joined but the corner is cut into the block and the joints are parallel to the adjoining stones. CP-43.

metope. Flat or ornamented slab between the triglyphs in the frieze of a Doric entablature. OM-86, OM-105.

miter. A joint between two units cut at angles that, when combined, equal the final angle. WA-21.

modillion. A usually scrolled bracket supporting a cornice. If undecorated, it is a block modillion. OM-71, OM-103.

molding. A shaped member, usually ornamental, used to accent an architectural element and to conceal construction joints. OM-64.

mosaic. A design composed of small units called tesserae set in mortar. FA-69.

mosaic bond. Masonry bond composed of irregularly shaped stone with dressed face set with a consistent width mortar joint and used for either solid or veneer walls. Also called cobweb bond. *See also* bond. WA-122.

mosaic tile. Tile with a surface area of less than 6 square inches (39 square centimeters). FP-93.

mud wall. *See* rammed.

muntin. A strip that is part of the framing structure holding glass panes in place in a window. WI-12.

mullion. A vertical member dividing door panels or multiple windows in a common frame. In contrast to a muntin it separates, rather than holding, the panels or panes. WI-12.

mutule. Flat block, usually decorated with guttae, under the soffit of a Doric corona, above the triglyph. OM-105.

necking. In classical architecture, the area between the bottom of the capital, and the top of the column shaft. CP-6.

nogging. Masonry that fills the open spaces of a timber-framed structure. GL-23.

oeil-de-boeuf. *See* bull's-eye window.

ogee. A double curve that forms an "S" shape. CR-134.

ogee arch. A pointed arch with S-shaped curves meeting in the center of the arch. CP-163.

ogee molding. *See* cyma.

order. In classical architecture, one of five groups of columns distinguished by similar entablatures, shafts, bases, and capitals. The orders are: Composite (or Compound), Corinthian, Doric, Ionic, Tuscan. *See also* individual entries.

oriel. A bay window that projects from an upper story. WI-79, GL-24.

ormolu. A gilt cast-bronze ornament. GL-25.

ovolo molding. Convex molding, elliptical or quarter-round in section. OM-70.

Palladian window. *See* serliana.

pantile. A roof tile that is S-shaped in section. When installed, the profile is parallel to the ridge with straight sides overlapping, giving a corrugated appearance. CR-45.

parapet. A low wall that may function as a guardrail at the edge of a balcony, roof, or terrace, sometimes with crenels. WA-161, WA-196.

parapet gable. A gable wall that extends past the roof line, often with an ornamental profile. CR-116.

parquetry. A flooring usually laid in a geometric pattern of contrasting materials or colors. FP-15.

patera. A circular ornament in shallow relief with a center element and, often, radiating flutes. *See also*

GL-20 Hipped roof

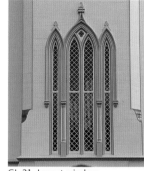

GL-21 Lancet window

GL-22 Mansard

GL-23 Nogging

GL-24 Oriel

GL-25 Ormolu

rosette. OM-62.

paver. A masonry unit intended for either pedestrian or vehicular traffic. FP-78, GL-26.

pavilion roof. A hipped roof with extremely steep slopes resulting in a very short, almost pointed ridge. CR-34, CR-35.

pebble dash. A variety of exposed aggregate in which pebbles are pressed or blown into the finish coat of stucco. Also called pebble wall. GL-3.

pedestal. The supporting structure beneath a column base. CP-63.

pediment. A low-pitched triangular, arched, or scrolled gable usually framed by molding. The resulting field may be decorated. *See also* scrolled pediment, segmental pediment. DW-73, GL-27.

pier. A vertical structural support, more massive than a post. CP-81.

pilaster. A nonstructural vertical element projecting from a building and rectangular in plan. While attached, it usually has the elements of a column. *See also* engaged column. CP-86, GL-28.

pitch. The slope or angle of a roof.

plain-sawn. A term describing lumber that has been cut from a log in strips. WA-6.

plinth. The bottom block of a column or pedestal. CP-33.

porte-cochère. A covered entry to a courtyard, large enough to allow for a vehicle. DW-82.

portico. An open entrance structure with a roof supported by columns. It may be attached as a porch or freestanding. CP-74.

post. A vertical structural support.

post-and-lintel. A term describing construction with horizontal members resting on load-bearing vertical members. Also called post-and-beam. CP-140.

quoin. (1) Masonry unit at the outside corner of a wall or window opening, emphasizing it by size, projection, rustication, or finish. WA-93, GL-29. (2) A brick cut for use as an exterior corner. WA-178.

rail. A horizontal unit in a frame.

rainwater head. A small, often decorated tank that collects rainwater from the gutter before it is discharged into the downspout. CR-157.

raked. A term describing a sloped architectural element: rake molding on the bargeboard of a gable, raking cornice on a pediment. WA-35.

rammed. A term describing a structure made by tightly packing earth between forms. WA-253.

random ashlar bond. Ashlar masonry laid without regular courses but with an overall effect of horizontal orientation. *See also* bond. WA-109.

reeding. Ornament consisting of a series of raised parallel lines. OM-1, OM-6.

relieving arch. A closed arch built over a lintel, window, or smaller open arch to divert the load from the member below. WA-107, WA-164.

return. The continuation of an architectural element around a corner—for example, the sides of a pilaster or molding that turns a corner.

reveal. The wall adjacent to a recessed window or door frame. *See also* soffit. WA-132.

ridge. The top of a pitched roof, where the two slopes meet. CR-73.

ridge cap. A protective cover over the joint formed at a roof ridge. CR-54.

rock face. A stone finish with emphasized face-plane shifts and rough corners, exaggerating the natural look of the stone. WA-68.

roof dormer. *See* dormer.

roof types. Terms that categorize roofs by the shapes resulting from their slopes and the intersections of their pitches—for example: *gable, gambrel, hipped, jerkinhead, mansard, pavilion, shed, terrace.* Several types may be combined. *See also* individual entries.

rosette. Circular ornament in low relief with floral petals radiating from a circular center. GL-30.

rose window. A circular window with tracery radiating from a center design. WI-67.

roundel. Small circular window, panel, or niche.

rowlock. A brick placed in the course in a vertical header position. *See also* brick. WA-166.

rubble. Stone consisting of fieldstone and irregular or partly dressed stone, often with one split or roughly finished face. WA-73, GL-31.

running. A term describing a motif or unit that repeats horizontally. FA-118.

running bond. A structural masonry bond formed when all units are laid in stretcher position, with a half-unit overlap. *See also* bond. WA-113.

rusticated. A term describing stone masonry with a recessed cut margin, so a channel is formed when the blocks are aligned. WA-112.

saltbox roof. A gabled roof with a much longer back than front slope. CR-121.

Salomonic column. A column with a spiral shaft. The shaft is twisted, in contrast to a column with ornament applied in a spiral band. CP-60.

sand finish. A stone finish that is granular and moderately smooth, varying with the characteristics of the specific stone. WA-75.

sash. The frame holding glass panes with muntins, mullions, or cames in a window. It may slide, swing, pivot, or be fixed.

sawn face. A term describing stone exhibiting the marks left by the saw used to cut it. WA-93.

sawtooth. A masonry or shingle course with units set on an angle but in the same plane as the face, producing a flat, serrated edge. WA-266.

scagliola. An imitation of marble or stone produced by mixing stone dust with a binder and coloring to imitate veining, grain, or other features. When hardened, the surface is polished.

Scamozzi capital. *See* angular capital.

scotia. A concave molding, quarter-round in section, with the lower part of the quarter-round extended. CP-34.

screen wall. (1) A brick wall with a pattern of open spaces between bricks in the courses. WA-167. (2) Concrete blocks made with open spaces that form a pattern when assembled. WA-229.

scrolled pediment. A broken segmental pediment with the top profile forming scrolls. GL-32.

segmental pediment. An arched rather than triangular pediment. WI-104.

serliana. A window, entrance, or blind opening consisting of two vertical flat-topped openings connected by a central arch forming a third opening. The side units are often framed by columns or pilasters, and topped with entablatures. An example is a Palladian window. WI-54.

sgraffito. A decorative plaster technique in which darker plaster is applied over a coat of lighter plaster and a design is scratched into the top coat, exposing the undercoat. FA-87.

shaft. The body of a column between the capital and

GL-26 Paver

GL-27 Pediment

GL-28 Pilaster

GL-29 Quoin

GL-30 Rosette

GL-31 Rubble

GL-32 Scrolled pediment

the base or pedestal.

shed roof. A roof with a single slope connecting a higher wall with a lower one. CR-55.

side light. A fixed-light window, usually vertically oriented, beside a door. DW-81.

single-hung window. *See* window.

skip-trowel. A plaster or stucco finish applied with visible trowel marks, sometimes forming a pattern. WA-246.

sill. (1) In a timber-framed wall, the bottom horizontal timber to which the posts are joined. (2) The bottom horizontal element of a doorway or window. Also called cill, sole, sule.

soffit. The finished underside of an exposed architectural element such as a beam or the ceiling of a staircase. OM-105.

soldier. A brick placed in a course in a vertical position, with the edge used as the face. *See also* brick. WA-202.

spandrel. (1) The area between the top of a window of a lower story and the bottom of the window above. WA-136. (2) The triangular shape between adjoining arches. CP-144, GL-33.

springer. The lowest stone in the curved portion of an arch. GL-34.

split face. A stone finish exhibiting the natural quarry texture resulting from splitting the stone. WA-58.

stack bond. A masonry bond formed when there is no overlapping of units and all vertical and horizontal joints are aligned. *See also* bond. WA-205.

standing seam. The joining of two planes of sheet metal in a folded seam perpendicular to the surface covered. CR-35.

stile. A vertical unit of a frame, such as a window sash or door frame.

straight joint. A term describing tiles installed with all the joints aligned. FP-60.

stretcher. A brick placed in a course with the longest dimension in the horizontal plane and the edge facing out. *See also* brick. WA-170.

strip windows. Horizontal bands of windows, usually single panes with few mullions, producing the effect of a strip of glass and primarily used in contemporary commercial architecture. WI-88.

stucco. A concrete plaster, often permanently colored, used to coat exterior walls. WA-251.

surbased arch. An arch rising less than half its span. CP-159.

terrace roof. *See* flat roof

tessera (pl. tesserae). A small piece of marble, stone, tile, glass, or other material used in mosaics. FP-103.

terrazzo. A floor treatment made from stone or glass chips in a matrix usually poured in place, between metal or plastic divider strips, then ground and polished smooth. Rustic terrazzo uses larger aggregate and the surface matrix is washed to expose the aggregate. FP-90, GL-35.

tile. A surfacing unit less than 12 inches (305 mm) square, usually relatively thin in relation to its face area.

timber frame. A wood frame construction in which the spaces are filled with brick, plaster, or similar material. WA-10.

toothing. Courses of stones or bricks that project from the wall, with spaces between the units. CP-90.

torus. A convex molding, semicircular in section.

CP-31.

trabeated. A term describing post-and-lintel construction. CP-133.

tracery. Panels, screens, or windows divided by shaped ribs, pierced ornament, or foils that form usually geometric patterns in a pointed arch or circular panel. Blind tracery is used as applied ornament. WI-67, GL-36.

transom. (1) Horizontal bar above a door that separates the door from a fanlight or panel. (2) A window in the transom.

transom light. A horizontal fixed light or working window above a door or window. DW-63.

triglyph. In a Doric frieze, a block with three vertical grooves that flanks the metopes. OM-84, OM-86.

trompe l'oeil. A decorative technique meaning "fool the eye." Usually a realistic painting, it may imitate a surface such as wood grain or marble. DW-8.

Tuscan order. The group of columns, capitals, and entablatures characterized by simple molding, unfluted columns, and no decoration. DW-81

tympanum. The face of a pediment, often ornamented. CP-156.

uncoursed rubble. Fieldstone set in mortar in random arrangement. Also called rough rubble. WA-288.

vault. (1) An arch that is deeper than the width it spans. Types include: *barrel, fan, groin.* (2) The architectural space enclosed by a vault. GL-37.

Venetian arch. Semicircular arch framing two openings separated by a column with a roundel above the column. CP-91.

vermiculation. A stone texture of incised, wormlike shapes, generally of equal size. WA-92.

Vitruvian scroll. An ornamental band consisting of repeated stylized waves. OM-35.

volute. A spiral scroll. CP-5.

voussoir. A wedge-shaped block that is a component of an arch. The angle of the wedge is determined by the arch's radius. WA-116.

wall dormer. A dormer on the same plane as the wall below. CR-85, CR-97.

waney-edged. A term describing wood siding with one unmilled, irregular edge that is exposed when installed. Originally applied to wood difficult to mill, such as elm, where the edge was left uncut for ease of production, the term now describes any siding with a rustic, irregular edge. WA-8.

water-table course. A masonry projection on an outside wall, slanted to keep water from running down the wall. WA-165.

weathering steel. Steel chemically treated to weather to a certain condition and then remain relatively stable, maintaining the visual effect of weathering without becoming unsound. DW-54.

window nomenclature. Windows are described by the number of lights (panes) per sash—for example, four-over-four means both sashes are divided into four lights; four-over-one means there are four lights in the top and one in the bottom sash. *See also* double-hung. WI-55.

window casing. *See* casing.

window frame. Two vertical members connected by two horizontal members and attached to the structure around the opening in a wall to house the sash or provide structure for hinges or pivots. It is often covered by casing.

GL-33 Spandrel

GL-34 Springer

GL-35 Terrazzo

GL-36 Tracery

GL-37 Vault

BIBLIOGRAPHY AND RESEARCH SOURCES

American Architecture: An Illustrated Encyclopedia. Cyril M. Harris. New York: W. W. Norton & Company, 1998.

American House Styles: A Concise Guide. John Milnes Baker. New York: W. W. Norton & Company, 1994.

The Architecture of Japan. Arthur Drexler. New York: The Museum of Modern Art, 1955

The Architecture Traveler: A Guide to 263 Key American Buildings. Sydney LeBlanc. New York: W. W. Norton & Company, 2005.

ArchitectureWeek: The New Magazine of Design and Building. www.ArchitectureWeek.com.

Architecture Woodwork Quality Standards, 8th ed. Reston, VA: the Architectural Woodwork Institute, 2003.

Building Construction Illustrated, Francis D. K. Ching. New York: Van Nostrand Reinhold Company, 1975.

The Classical Orders of Architecture. Robert Chitham. New York: Rizzoli, 1985.

Construction Glossary. J. Stewart Stein. New York: John Wiley and Sons, 1980.

Dictionary of Architecture. James Stevens Curl. Oxford: Oxford University Press, 1999.

Dictionary of Architecture and Construction, 2nd ed. Cyril Harris. New York: McGraw-Hill, 1993

The Encyclopedia of Decorative Arts: 1890-1940. Philippe Garner. New York: Van Nostrand Reinhold Company, 1978

The Elements of Style, rev. ed. Stephen Calloway, Elizabeth Cromley, editors. New York: Simon & Schuster, 1996.

Glossary of Stone Industry Terms. Building Stone Institute. Itasca, IL: Building Stone Institute, 1997.

A Guide to Paving. AJ McCormack and Son. http://www.pavingexpert.com/home.htm.

A History of Architecture. Spiro Kostof. New York: Oxford University Press, 1985.

Illustrated Dictionary of Building Materials and Techniques. Paul Bianchina. Blue Ridge Summit, PA: Tab Books, 1986.

Katachi: Classical Japanese Design. Takeji Iwamiya and Kazuya Takaoka. San Francisco: Chronicle Books, 1999.

The Masonry Glossary. International Masonry Institute, M. Patricia Cronin, editor. Boston: CBI Publishing Company, 1981.

Pictorial Encyclopedia of Historical Architectural Plans, Details and Elements. John Theodore Haneman. New York: Dover Publications, 1984.

Pictorial Glossary: Architecture. The Heritage Education Network (THEN). http://histpres.mtsu.edu/then/Architecture/index.html.

Tile Glossary. Interceramic. http://www.interceramicusa.com/us/en/products/ti/tile glossary.asp.

A Visual Dictionary of Architecture. Frank Ching. New York: Van Nostrand Reinhold Company, 1995.

The Woodworker's Reference Guide and Sourcebook. John L. Feirer. New York: Charles Scribner's Sons, 1983.

PHOTO CREDITS

Austin, Patterson, Disston
376 Pequot Avenue
Southport, CT 06890
203-255-4031
   and
4 Midland Street
Quogue, NY 11959
631-653-1481
www.apdarchitects.com

Meredith Barchat
For picture information: www.stocksurfaces.com

Roger Bartels Architects
27 Elizabeth Street
Norwalk, CT 06854
203-838-5517
www.rogerbartelsarchitects.com

Dobyan & Dobyan Builders
Fairfield, CT 06824
203-395-8553.

Guy Gurney
P.O. Box 1227
Darien, CT 06820
203-656-6652
www.guygurney.com

Duane Langenwalter
477 Main Street, Suite 204
Monroe, CT 06468-1139
www.outofthinair.com

The Lockwood-Mathews Mansion Museum
295 West Avenue
Norwalk, CT 06850
203 838-9799

Peter Miller
For picture information: www.stocksurfaces.com

The Preservation Society of Newport County
424 Bellevue Avenue
Newport, RI 02840
401-847-1000

ABOUT THE CD-ROM

The accompanying CD-ROM contain the glossary and printable JPEG files of all the images in the book.

With the appropriate graphics software, the CD images can be used by artists and designers in developing concepts, preparing presentations for clients, and communicating visual information to others. Although the images are primarily intended for on-screen display, they can also be printed on either a black and white or color printer.

Further information about the image formats can be found on the readme.txt file on the CD.

The images and text in this book and on the CD-ROM are the property of the author or the individuals or organizations listed in the photo credits and may not be used commercially without their express permission.

All images except those credited otherwise are copyright © 2005 Judy Juracek. Original images may be obtained by contacting the author through www.stocksurfaces.com, or write to P.O. Box 1227, Darien, CT 06820.